The Global Volunteer

Free Travel Opportunities to Help Abroad with Gap Year Programs, The Peace Corps, WWOOF and More

Ryan Scott Shannon

ISBN: 9798643529941

CONTENTS

Travel Volunteering: You Can Have Your Cake and Eat It, Too!

If you're travel-obsessed like me, you're always dreaming of far-off places to visit. Maybe you want to explore the lush tropical vibes of Bali or help orphans learn English in a rural village in Guatemala. There are just so many exciting places to see! Unfortunately, not all of us have the bank account to do so. What's worse is when searching for travel volunteer programs, you've likely come across borderline scam websites that charge hundreds - or maybe even thousands - just for a week or two of volunteering. That's not what this book is about. I've sifted through countless websites and resources to find you the best ways to see more of the world while helping others for close to $0! If you're looking for a fulfilling program to fill your gap year or are looking to take a sabbatical in a meaningful way, you'll find what you're looking for in the contents of this book - and you'll save big on accommodation and living expenses in the process!

Wait...$0? How Is It Possible to Travel for Free as a Volunteer?

To answer your question right off the bat: yes, it's completely possible to travel the world for free with volunteer programs! There are government-sponsored programs that cover everything you need and the vast majority of "Helper Exchange" programs offer you room and board for free. You may or may not have to cover airfare for yourself, and of course, if you're planning on buying souvenirs and eating out in restaurants - it'll be you footing the bill! However, if you're focused on travel alone and don't have an expensive lifestyle (i.e. you don't need to buy a new pair of shoes every month and don't pick up every exotic trinket you see) then you can get away with traveling completely free or for less than $100 per month or so (including transportation). If you budget smart, live within your means, and find the right programs or helper exchanges, you may just spend $0 for the entirety of your travels.

Before we dig into things, I want to introduce myself. My name is Ryan Shannon and I've been traveling the world since I was 18 years old. Since then, I've visited 24 countries and even finished my Bachelor's degree in Turin, Italy (which I'll explain in another book. Getting a student visa is a great way to see the world in-depth for a longer time!) When I was younger, I was addicted to the Travel Channel and would find myself looking for flights to far-away, exotic locations for fun. Then I became an adult and realized: 'My life is in my hands! I'm going to be one of those crazy people that chases after fulfilling my dreams rather than counting zeroes in my bank account!' And so, I took off and traveled the world in a typical vagabond style. I slept overnight in airports, I stayed in divey hostels, and I was even selected for the prestigious National Security Language Initiative for Youth program to be a youth ambassador in India and study Hindi and Urdu. My life so far has been rich and meaningful - and it's mostly because of my travels. Because of this, I wanted to share with others how they can travel the world for free or incredibly low cost as I have.

I've split this little book into two main sections so that it's easy for you to find the opportunities to travel the world you find most interesting! Those sections are:

- **Volunteer Experiences.** When you do a little good for others, a little good comes back to you (namely in the form of room and board!) I've broken down all kinds of non-scammy programs like WWOOFing, Americorps, The Peace Corps, and at the end have included 50+ resources that allow you to travel free as a tour leader, English teacher and even as a turtle rescuer! No matter what your interests or skills are, you can rest assured there's likely an opportunity around the world where you can put them to use to help others.
- **Donations and In-Kind.** Travel is a life-transforming experience and because of that, many of your friends and family would be willing to give you a few dollars here and there to make your dreams of traveling the world come true. And if you're adventurous and in for a real immersive experience, you may opt for Couchsurfing where you live like a local in a stranger's home. If you're new to travel that may sound crazy, but it's something I've done seven times now and it's allowed me to get a real, local experience and make lifelong friends along the way! Plus, when you use these methods you can find volunteer opportunities on-site.

When I Say Free Do I Really Mean Free?

As the saying goes: if it's too good to be true, it probably is. Let me be clear from the start: when I say $0, I mean you won't have to spend any money once you get to your destination (if you're participating in a short-term volunteer exchange, for example, you'll likely be expected to pay for your own transportation. In some cases, if a flight or bus ticket isn't outrageously expensive, you can negotiate with hosts and see if they're willing to cover it. Some may pay for your trip - especially if you're planning on helping long-term). That'll save you hundreds or thousands of dollars each month as you travel around the world. Another thing I want to make clear is that these experiences I've outlined in detail below are free in the monetary sense. What you will be paying with is your time, commitment to cultural exchange, acts of service and education. Since cost is the biggest deterrent to traveling the world, I wanted to answer this common question right off the bat. So, yes, you can travel for free, but you may have some negligible expenses that can range from paying for a meal or two each day to paying for your own bus fare, etc.

Will Room and Board Be Covered?

In the vast majority of cases, yes! If you're selected for some of the government-sponsored programs , everything will be covered for you - flight and all. In the case of help exchanges, I've found that most hosts do offer at least a few meals each day in addition to the free room (and really, paying for just one or two meals per day isn't all that expensive - especially if you're helping or WWOOFing in a country with a high cost of living. The free accomodation helps tremendously to offset your costs).

What Expenses Will I Have to Cover?

- **Travel Insurance.** As they say, it's better to be safe than sorry. If you're planning on traveling to multiple countries, be sure to find a travel insurance plan that covers you anywhere and everywhere you go. Travel insurance protects you in all kinds of scenarios: from illness to missed flights to stolen luggage. For those staying long-term in a country, you may be eligible for their national healthcare.

- **Medical Bills.** Going hand-in-hand with insurance, you'll need to pay for your own medical bills. When you have insurance, your bills will be greatly reduced. In some countries, you may even be able to pay for a trip to the hospital out of pocket (as I did, for example when I accidentally jammed a Q-tip in my ear in Croatia. Embarrassing, but true! I only paid $30 out of pocket and was surprisingly seen in less than 5 minutes).
- **Transportation.** In some of the programs, you'll need to cover airfare or fare for the bus. But this doesn't just go for long-haul trips; if you're planning on moving around a city or town, you'll need to pay the fare for the bus or metro. Keep that in mind and budget accordingly.
- **Food.** Again, in many cases food is provided (or at least a meal or two each day). If you've found an irresistible helper exchange, for example, that doesn't include food you'll need to leave room in your budget for food. This can be dirt cheap in countries like Thailand and India, or quite expensive if in Switzerland, for example.

Why You Need to Travel Right Now

As much as I love my grandma, it's no secret that getting around is a lot easier for a 20-something year old than a 70-something year old. I'm able to run for the metro and slip inside before the doors close, climb to the top of ancient bell towers and move around freely. While I may not have the experience and knowledge of somebody older than me, I do have my youth and plan on utilizing the gift of my young, able body now. I'm able to get around without any problems and it's safe to say that my health is at or nearing its peak. If you're like me in your 20's or 30's, you need to make travel a priority. When I'm on my own, I'm able to get to where I need to be on foot (or even before since I'm a power walker!) the time stated on Google Maps. When you're traveling with or are an older person, it's no surprise that it can take a bit longer. While there's a certain beauty in taking things in slow and stopping to smell the roses along the way, when you need to hustle to catch a flight or hop on the bus it's much more difficult when you are older. Logistics become a bit more complex. When I travel with my grandma, I don't think for myself but for her: if we've been walking a lot, I try to find an elevator. If we're waiting for a bus or metro, I might let the first pass and hope the second is less crowded. I may be more vigilant in areas known for pickpocketing or petty crime since older people are often targeted. I don't want to put off any older people reading this: you can travel the world (and you absolutely should!) but it's no surprise travel for you is different from a 20-something year old. Many of these options are open to older people (like WWOOFing, Helper Exchanges and even the Senior Corps) so that you can give back to local communities and see more of the world.

The point is: try to seize the day and take advantage of your youth. Travel now instead of putting it off for later. As we all know, later can easily become never. Tomorrow is often the busiest day of the week, as it's said. Don't put your dreams off until tomorrow. Take proactive steps toward achieving your dreams to travel the world and work towards it every single day. When you're thinking of staying complacent and watching Netflix rather than finishing this book and looking into some of the programs I've outlined: ask yourself which option is going to make your most proud and fulfilled in the next few years. Your everyday actions cultivate the person you are. If your goal is traveling the world, make sure that's the center of your life and where you are directing your efforts and energy. You are capable of making that leap and booking that one way ticket. Not to get all new age spiritual on you, but the universe is on your side! Choose to take actions that lead to lasting fulfilment rather than temporary comfort.

Reality Check: Travel Is Different from Vacationing

One thing to make clear: this is about travel and living a life full of adventure, not of comfort (not that you won't be provided with a comfortable place to stay. It's just that it likely won't come with any frills). Traveling and living a life on the go, hopping from place to place, country to country was an integral part of my life (though I'm now learning that I prefer to stay put in one place for a few weeks to a few months for an immersive experience rather than "fast travel"). But, I'm not exactly on 'vacation'. Traveling to me is a completely different concept than vacationing. Vacations are about enjoying the same amenities as you would back home, talking with the same people and remaining comfortable, never daring to step outside of your comfort zone. Travel, on the other hand is a journey. Sometimes you just have to go with the flow and take risks. It can be scary and intimidating at first, but I promise once you're on a plane en route to the location of your dreams, it will completely change your life. Travelling is more about being immersed in a foreign culture, living life fast but taking in the moments slow. Living more like a local and less like a tourist. Don't expect to be living a lavish lifestyle, sleeping in fancy resorts and having all of the comforts of home wherever you are in the world. As I mentioned, I have spent several nights sleeping at the airport, catching the bus like a local, and carrying only the items I need in either my backpack or carry-on (just a few of the methods I have used to save money).

As somebody who has traveled to dozens of countries and numerous cities domestically in the United States, I have learned how to travel completely self-sufficiently, all on my own dime. No, I do not live a glamorous life (in fact, I have just enough clothes to fit inside a carry-on suitcase) and I almost never eat out. I don't see the value in having an expensive wardrobe, and my most valuable (in a monetary sense) possession is my cellphone I got on sale for €140 euros. When I travel, I don't expect to be dining out at 5-star restaurants every night and going on overrated, overpriced guided tours. Instead I go into each new destination with an open mind and focus more on the intangible rather than the tangible. A little creativity, open-mindedness and flexibility goes a long way if you want your travel experience to not be stressful and eye-opening. I consider myself a basic and minimalist type of person, unattached to my possessions. I live simply so that I can simply travel the world and live for what I love. And that is my philosophy to travel that I would like to teach to you. Travel is about being spontaneous and focusing on the beautiful things in life rather than working towards trivial things that don't matter like money and the conventional definition of success.

Who This Book Is For

- **High School Students.** Being a high schooler is an exciting time! These are some of the most transformative, life-determining years. You really have an opportunity to figure out what type of person you want to be and pursue your interests. If you're interested in traveling the world - don't pass up these opportunities. Not only will programs like WWOOF and AmeriCorps look great on a college application and resume, they'll completely change your life (and best of all you and your parents won't have to spend a dime if selected).
- **Gap Year.** You've put in thirteen long years of study and now it's come to an end. You'll find most of your peers will go straight into the workforce or college, but there is another option: traveling the world. After spending so much time inside a classroom, maybe it's time to learn outside of the classroom from people and places that are completely unknown to you. There are plenty of gap year programs available to high school graduates - and you don't have to spend thousands of dollars

on them as some companies would lead you to be. Find out how you can organize your own trip to volunteer in a dog shelter in Spain or become in Au Pair in France, among many other exciting opportunities.

- **College Students.** Whether you're already enrolled in a university and want to kill two birds with one stone (travel and education), or haven't started your academic career yet and are considering getting an international degree as I did, you'll find out how you can pair your need for education with your wanderlust.
- **Retirees.** As I mentioned above, there are some challenges for older people who want to travel (just as there are for younger folks i.e. money) but that shouldn't stop you from seeing the world. Many farms may be looking for your expertise in gardening or cooking via WWOOFing, or you may be able to volunteer in an orphanage in Latin America, for example, through a help exchange program. On top of that, there are also organizations you can join within the US like the Senior Corps which allows you to make a difference in a different corner of the US. Whether you have your eye set on an exotic, international destination or want to see more of the US, there are plenty of opportunities for you to explore.
- **Young Couples.** Sometimes two is better than one! If you want to travel the world as a pair, there are a plethora of benefits. In fact, you'll save on your WWOOFing membership (which costs between $20 and $60 in most cases. A little expense for a lot of travel and free room and board!)

Travel is not limited to the elite, the privileged and the "lucky." If you want to travel - you will! Carve out your own future and live the life of your dreams by finding programs that allow you to travel for free. I've provided you with countless programs and sincerely hope you take advantage of all the resources and opportunities at your disposal. There's so much of the world to see and so little time! Keep reading to find out how your dream to travel can soon become reality.

National and International Volunteer Experiences

You can help make the grass a little greener on the other side by participating in international volunteer experiences as you travel the world - best of all, this can be your golden ticket to travel free. There are so many places and people in need of volunteers - and they're not just in Africa or poor parts of Asia, either. The fact is, poverty and need can strike anywhere; even in "rich" countries in Western Europe, the United States, Australian and other Western countries. In this section, you'll find many types of ways to help - from small businesses starting out who need a helping hand (e.g. hostels, restaurants and farms), to parents looking for a break or needing a mother-tongue language speaker to teach their kids (e.g. Au Pair, nannying, etc.), to established organizations that could use specific skills (like the PeaceCorps and Americorps) to benefit developing communities. The point is people are in need everywhere; not just in poor parts of the world. And you can make a difference. In this section, I'll teach you how to find the right opportunities and use the best resources to get connected with people who need your help.

Pair Your Passion for Helping Other with World Travel

Not only will volunteer programs and exchanges abroad allow you to see more of the world, you'll also feel better about yourself and make a difference in local communities, too. Some people may not feel ethical choosing the volunteer route *just* to travel for free, which is fine. But in reality, you're paying with your time and can make a difference in others' lives - whether it's just a small family or an entire community looking for your business expertise or skills in healthcare. You'll be volunteering for around 20 hours per week (or more), which should earn you more than just room and board if you were actually employed in a paid position (depending on where you are and the cost of living). You don't necessarily need to be passionate about spaying and neutering dogs, for example, however that shouldn't stop you from applying to help at a non-profit that 'fixes' cats and dogs. Your passion may come with time - or, not at all. But, at least you're doing something important in exchange for free room (and usually board). When you embark on your international volunteer experience, you'll learn more about yourself than you imagined possible. Before you start your learning experience, it's important to decide which route you want to take: do you want to go with a formal government-sponsored program, or volunteer independently?

State-sponsored Volunteer Programs VS. Independent Help Exchanges

As you'll read, there are two types of volunteer programs: state-sponsored programs (like AmeriCorps and PeaceCorps) and independent help exchanges (like reaching an agreement with a family, business, hostel or school on Helpx.net, Workaway.info or on other travel exchange websites). In general, with state-sponsored options, you'll need to fill out an application and potentially be interviewed. The process is more formal and detailed than simply messaging families and businesses on independent help exchange websites (as you would on HelpX.net or Workaway.info). The process can take much longer to complete, whereas with independent help exchanges, you can arrange an agreement in just a few messages on Whatsapp or Facebook (though I do recommend you meet virtually on Skype before packing your bags to make sure the opportunity is a good fit for both you and the host). An advantage to going through a government-sponsored volunteer program is you can take advantage of the "name factor". Almost everyone has heard of AmeriCorps and the PeaceCorps, which thinking ahead would be a great boost to your professional profile. You can easily add your experience to your resume and LinkedIn this way, whereas when you go the independent route you'll likely have to explain things further since the organization or private business you help won't be as well-known.

Find Out How You Can Volunteer (And Get Free Room and Board!)

In this section I'll go over some of the most common, reputable ways to travel around the world through volunteer exchange programs. At the end of this chapter, I've also compiled a **mega list** of other volunteer opportunities (e.g. leading tours, working on a cruise ship, providing medical care and more!) for you to make a difference in another part of the world.

- **WWOOFing.** Discover how you can help farmers around the world raise sustainable crops and livestock focusing on sustainability and green practices.
- **Help Exchange Programs (HelpX and Workaway).** Find the right opportunity to help families and small business owners around the world. Common positions include teaching English, farming, working in a hostel and nannying.
- **Americorps.** Americorps provides fantastic opportunities for young adults to get involved in their communities. I'll be going

over the three branches within AmeriCorps and even cover the Senior Corps.

- **The Peace Corps.** If you want to make a difference on a global scale, it's time to join the Peace Corps. You've probably heard of this program - find out if it's a match for you.
- **Plus 50+ Volunteer Programs in the US and Abroad.** The opportunities are endless! I've given you access to over 50 programs - from helping preserve wildlife in Australia to protecting sea turtles in Mexico, you'll be sure to find an opportunity for you!

Instead of wasting hundreds of dollars on room and board each month, why not travel for free in exchange for roughly 20 hours of work each week? You may even make some friends, learn a new language and develop new skills along the way! With so many opportunities available, I'm sure you'll find something that fits what you're looking for in your dream destination. Pick out a few of your favorites and start applying or sending messages to get the ball rolling!

World Wide Opportunities on Organic Farms (WWOOFing)

Skills Needed	Most skills can be learned on the job, however a background in sustainability, farming and gardening is a major plus. You'll also need to be reasonably fit and comfortable working outside.
Hours Per Week	Varies per host and country. You will have to negotiate this yourself. Expect to work 20-40 hours per week.
Requirements and Restrictions	Ages 18+ for most countries. You must have a valid visa for the country you're planning on WWOOFing in.
Location	Worldwide excluding about half of the African countries and the Middle East.

Get ready to get your hands dirty and dig in! WWOOFing (the act of farming via the World Wide Opportunities on Organic Farms) grants eager volunteers the opportunity to support organic farmers around the world. What's WWOOF all about? WWOOF's mission statement sums it up perfectly: "WorldWide Opportunities on Organic Farms, (WWOOF) is part of a worldwide movement linking visitors with organic farmers and growers to promote cultural and educational experiences based on trust and non-monetary exchange thereby helping to build a sustainable global community." Since organic farmers often do not receive subsidies from the government (unlike conventional farmers, who usually use carcinogenic chemicals like Glyphosate, also known as 'RoundUp') they need all the help they can get from people like you. There are a variety of ways you can offer your hand in farming: from harvesting fresh produce, to picking berries, to making wine and cheese. WWOOFing is a great way to connect with nature and see first-hand how our food supply is produced.

There are thousands upon thousands of hosts looking for workers to stay on their farms and lend a helping hand. The tricky part is, however, you have to apply by country and pay a membership for each nation's WWOOFing organization you join i.e. there isn't a global WOOFing page where you can browse and compare all WWOOFing opportunities side by side. That means if you want to WWOOF for one month in France, another in Italy and another in Spain, you will have to pay separate fees to each of the countries' WWOOFing organizations. But don't let that deter you from enjoying the benefits WWOOFing has to offer! While it may seem complex at first, becoming a WWOOFer is a great way to see the world while helping locals produce fresh, nutrient-dense food for their local communities - and paying the fees for each country is a fraction of what you'd be paying compared to what you'd pay in accomodation and food.

What Types of Ways Can You Help as a WWOOFer?

- **Sowing seeds.** If you're WWOOFing in spring, chances are you'll be helping scatter seeds.

- **Making compost.** The great thing about organic farms is that little is wasted; everything from food scraps to grass clippings usually end up in compost.
- **Gardening and planting.** As the name suggests, you'll likely be doing some agricultural farming during your experience. From planting raspberry stalks to pulling weeds, you'll have a varied experience and learn what it takes to go from farm to table.
- **Chopping wood.** Not so glamorous, but a great workout!
- **Milking goats and cows.** If you want real milk that's free of synthetic hormones the way nature intended, you've got to WWOOF at a dairy farm and taste the difference for yourself.
- **Baking bread.** Many WWOOF hosts require WWOOFers to help make baked goods for sale in cafes and supermarkets.
- **Construction.** From revamping a greenhouse to building raised garden beds, if you're good with your hands a construction-oriented opportunity is right for you.
- **Kitchen help.** If you're tired of working on the farm, but your skills in the kitchen to work!
- **Selling at Farmers Markets.** Not only do WWOOFers work on the farm, many also help sell at Farmers Markets, which is a great way to practice your sales skills and adds a nice boost to your resume.
- **And more!** The opportunities are varied when you become a WWOOFer. I encourage you to browse the listings and see for yourself what kinds of things you can do. There are tons of other activities I didn't mention like beekeeping, care for sheep and alpacas, and creating organic skincare products. Explore your opportunities with WWOOF!

What You Need to Know Before Becoming a WWOOFer

What's it like when you become a WWOOFer? For just 4-6 hours of work per day, you will be provided with food and accommodation (not a bad deal!). Just note that the required working hours as well as room and board varies from host to host so you'll have to sort through each listing individually. But in general, you can expect to work around 20 hours per week. Think about it as a part-time job in exchange for a free place to stay and delicious organic cuisine! Some hosts will give you multiple days off while others may only give you one. Some may not provide food (most do) while others may provide breakfast, lunch and dinner. Since it can vary so much from host to host, be sure to read the listings carefully and ask questions to the host to make sure it's the right fit for you.

One of the best things about WWOOFing is that the types of work are endless within the agricultural sector, and the hosts are just as diverse. With one host, you may be picking berries on a farm, staying in the guest bedroom in a huge farmhouse. Another time, you may be working in sugar cane fields and staying in a tent in Hawaii. It all depends; there are so many great options to be discovered (it's sure to be a journey!). Most volunteers stay for 1-2 weeks, but the total amount of time and hours worked is totally negotiable and something that fits your needs is sure to be worked out. If you and a host really hit it off, you may even be able to stay on a long-term basis. The bottom line is: if you're interested in seeing what it takes to produce healthy, nutritious food while having the opportunity to explore your surroundings in a different country, WWOOFing is for you!

While WWOOFing is a highly recommended way of traveling the world for free, there are some drawbacks to take into consideration before you make the commitment. As mentioned, you do have to pay a fee to join (but again, this is a small price to pay considering you're given a free place to stay - and a potentially life-changing experience). WWOOF is organized on a national level (so you have to create and pay a fee for each country that you wish to WWOOF in), so that may be something to consider (i.e. your costs will be higher if you travel to multiple countries as a WWOOFer). But ultimately, being able to save the money in the long run makes WWOOFing worth it. Even if you buy multiple WWOOFing memberships for multiple countries, the price is usually less than what you'd pay for a night in a decent hotel!

Another thing is that since this is farm work, you will most likely be working in suburban or rural lands. This can be a blessing or a curse. If you need the hustle and bustle of city life, this may not be for you (though there are some urban farming movements that have sprouted! Pun intended). On the bright side, WWOOFing provides a way for you to challenge yourself and explore a different lifestyle that you may be accustomed to living as a city or suburb-dweller. It's a great program that allows you to explore authentic, small town cultures and unplug for a while and truly connect with the people around you. If you work online as a Digital Nomad (which you can learn about in my other book: Laptop Entrepreneur: Realistic Ways You Can Live the Dream Abroad as a Digital Nomad and Make Money Online. Read a copy after you finish this book!) WWOOFing is a great way to get out into the outdoors and recharge your batteries. Best of all, you can work online for a few hours each week to create an income as you WWOOF.

WWOOFing is a great experience everyone should partake at some point in their lifetime; rich or poor, young or old. The reality is we can't all own farms, but we can experience what it's like to grow quality, pesticide-free food. It allows you the opportunity to get your hands dirty and see what goes into producing the food we so often take for granted in our supermarkets. This is something I still have not yet done, but I am planning on WWOOFing soon. As much as I love being in the city and admiring various architectural styles, partaking in cultural events and getting lost in a crowd, there's something refreshing about disconnecting and getting a little dirty. If you're like me and feel at home in the country or want to try something different than what you're used to, give WWOOFing a go! WWOOFing is available in most of the world— just check out wwoof.net to find amazing opportunities in countries you've always dreamed of visiting!

WWOOFing Fees by Country

I've done the work so you don't have to! I've looked at each individual country's fee schedule and summarized it below. To give you an idea of how much you'd have to budget, here are a few countries and their annual fees (accurate as of March 12, 2020. Note the "*" denotes that there is no official WWOOF organization but is instead organized by WWOOF Independents):

The Americas

United States of America	$40 Single, $65 Joint
Chile	$40 Single, $55 Joint
Latin America* (Includes: Mexico, Colombia, Costa Rica, Belize, Ecuador, Venezuela, Guatemala, Peru)	$20
Canada	$50 Single, $75 Joint
Argentina*	£20.00 Single, £30.00 Joint
Brazil*	£20.00 Single, £30.00 Joint
Uruguay*	£20.00 Single, £30.00 Joint

Europe

France	€25 Single, €30 Joint

Italy	€35 Single *No joint rate available
Spain	€20 Single, €36 Joint
Portugal	€20 Single, €30 Joint *Valid for two years
United Kingdom	£20.00 Single, £30.00 Joint
Norway	€20 Single, €35 Joint *Valid for two years
The Netherlands	€20 Single, €30 Joint
Czechia (The Czech Republic)	€15 Single, €22 Joint
Austria	€25 Single, €37 Joint
Switzerland	CHF 19 Single, CHF 29 Joint
Ireland	€25 Single, €40 Joint
Greece	€29 Single, €49 Joint *Valid for two years
Germany	€25 Single
Denmark	€25 Single, €40 Joint
Sweden	€27 Single, €42 Joint *Valid for two years

Asia

Thailand	€47.8 Single
China	$50
India	$40 Single, $60 Joint

Philippines	$25 Single
Sri Lanka	$35 Single, $50 Joint
Israel	160 ILS Single, 270 ILS Joint

Africa

Nigeria	$50
Malawi	*Fee not specified
Sierra Leone	*Fee not specified
South Africa	*Fee not specified

Oceania

New Zealand	NZD$40 Single and Joint, NZD$20 Renewals
Australia	AUS$70 Single, AUS$120 Joint

WWOOFing isn't entirely free, but the opportunity to help improve local communities and farmers across the world is priceless. Not to mention, the plant will also benefit from your work, too, since WWOOF farmers do not use toxic chemicals like Glyphosate. Instead, they use sustainable farming techniques that add minerals back into the soil and focus on the Circular Economy rather than wasting precious resources. If you've got green thumbs - or want to see if you have them! - don't miss this opportunity.

Steps to Take to Start WWOOFing

- For a more in-depth look at what WWOOFing is and how you can get involved head to the "Getting Started" area of their website: http://wwoof.net. You'll also be able to explore their interactive map that pinpoints where hosts are located and whether they're a part of the official WWOOFing organization or are independently organized.

- Double-check visa requirements and make sure you're able to stay in the country you'd like to WWOOF in legally.
- Screen each potential host thoroughly. This doesn't mean you need to integrate them, but ask specific questions about the accomodation and ensure the hours you'll work and the types of jobs you'll be working are negotiated beforehand.
- Sort through some of the listings on the national WWOOF website of the country you'd like to visit. Figure out what types of opportunities sound best - do you want to work with animals? Or, would you prefer to grow fruits and vegetables?

Become a 'Helper' (Independent Volunteer Exchange)

Skills Needed	Varies from construction to gardening and farming, to art to managing a hotel, to cleaning or simply teaching someone a language.
Hours Per Week	0-25 hours on average in exchange for accommodation.
Requirements and Restrictions	Primarily limited to two options: HelpX.net and workaway.info, although there are arrangements you can make if you have connections. You can even join groups on Facebook and Couchsurfing to find helper opportunities, or even contact hostels directly. The registration fee for Workaway.info is EUR 29.00 for 1 year and EUR 20.00 for 2 years on HelpX.net. If you're looking for a childcare or nanny experience (Au

	Pair), these opportunities are almost all exclusively for females.
Location	Worldwide.

Being a Helper is just like being a WWOOFer (and in fact, there are many opportunities to help on farms as a Helper); the difference is, as a helper you're not limited to the field. You can help with everything from childcare to teaching private individuals your native language to working as a receptionist in a hotel. You'll find that the most common helper experiences are: at hostels, on farms and helping families with childcare or language learning. But that's not all! There are thousands of opportunities for you to choose from in virtually every country in the world (though the Helper communities are mostly located in the USA, Western European countries, Australia and New Zealand). You can expect to work around 20 hours per week as you would as a WWOOFer, but some hosts require zero formal hours; some may just want to host someone in their house as a cultural exchange or as a way to learn from a native speaker. It all depends; you'll have to look over the descriptions closely to find out how many hours are expected of you each week, whether you'll have any time off, etc. From HelpX.net: "[The] time range can vary considerably depending on the tasks at hand and the host's preferences. Some hosts may require just 2 hours per day for accommodation only, and ask you to provide and cook your own food. Others may expect 6 hours per day in return for meals, your own room and sometimes other benefits such as free Internet use, horse riding, kayaking, bikes, local sight-seeing trips, yoga or English lessons, etc. Some will give weekends off, while others might allow you to put in 8 hours one day and later take a full day off. Helpers often live with the host family and are expected to join in and offer a helping hand with day-to-day activities." In general, you're limited to two main websites to find host opportunities, though there are some other ways to connect with people and businesses looking for helpers (which I've explained in the following section).

How Do You Find Legitimate Helper Opportunities?

Entrusting someone you haven't met to house and usually feed you is a big deal. There are a few scam websites out there and flaky hosts; fortunately, the two websites I've listed below are legitimate and display reviews from past Helpers so you can feel more at ease. Your best resources for finding hosts looking for a helper include:

- **HelpX.net.** You'll be able to browse thousands of hosts scattered across the world. HelpX breaks the Helper opportunities into seven main categories: Organic Farmstay, Non-organic Farmstay, Homestay, Backpacker Hostel, Accomodation, Boat and Other. When you type the website in your browser and land on the page, you'll notice the website looks a bit dated. Don't let that scare you off; again, thousands of hosts and helpers are active there.
- **Workaway.info.** Workaya is the world's largest Helper Exchange network. When you land on the website (which is far easier to use than HelpX), you'll find thousands upon thousands of active hosts (in fact, there are over 40,000 hosts on WorkAway) looking for helpers like you. You'll be able to browse photos and reviews, too. They've made finding the right host easy by sorting them by location and opportunity type: Home Sitting, Animal Welfare and Pet Sitting, Communities, Boat, Sustainable Projects, Farmstays and more!
- **Au Pair Websites.** There's a huge demand for Au Pairs around the world. Since this option is almost exclusively limited to females and an entire book can be written on what it's like to be an Au Pair, I won't go into much depth with this option. That being said, there are plenty of Au Pair options you can find on

both HelpX and Workaway. Additionally, there are plenty of other reputable Au Pair websites (which I've included at the end of this section) for you to find the perfect family to help.

- **Facebook Groups.** Leveraging your Facebook account is a great way to connect with hosts looking for helpers. I won't go into too much detail with this option, however, since there is no review system in place and application system as there is with HelpX and Workaway. If you feel confident and are an experienced traveler, you can use Facebook groups to your advantage and find plenty of great opportunities to volunteer around the world. Try typing in keywords like 'Hostel volunteer,' 'Help exchange,' 'International volunteer,' 'Teach English abroad,' and other keywords along those lines. You'll find many hosts will post positions - don't be shy, message them!
- **Couchsurfing Groups.** Couchsurfing also has groups that you can join and take advantage of too. You can use those same keywords above for Facebook on Couchsurfing. The advantage of using both Facebook and Couchsurfing is that they're both free to use (unlike Workaway and HelpX which both have a relatively small fee). On top of that, your Couchsrufing profile should be complete if you want Couchsurfing hosts to allow you to stay with them. This works to your advantage because you already have plenty of information on your Couchsurfing profile that hosts looking for helpers can read to feel you out. If you want a free option to find Helper opportunities, Couchsurfing is a great community to be a part of.
- **Personal Connections.** If you have any friends or family friends with accommodation businesses around the world, you may be able to reach an agreement with them. In exchange for a free place to stay, you can help as a receptionist or with cleaning. Be open minded and receptive - you never know who

you'll meet and an opportunity to stay somewhere for free in exchange for a bit of work may present itself.

Typical Helper Opportunities

There are thousands of needs to fulfill on these volunteer exchange websites. You'll quickly see you have thousands of opportunities to make a difference across the world in all kinds of different fields. From a family simply looking for somebody to interact with in English (or German, French and Spanish. These are also common languages that are in-demand) to single moms looking for a babysitter and someone to pick their kids up from school, to farmwork, to business experts and remodelers. There are several different options to choose from so you get a great fit for what you're looking for. Best of all, you'll be able to explore new interests completely risk-free. Take farming, for example. I studied Business and Management in university, but I'm very much drawn to sustainable practices and green living, including low to zero waste ways of organic farming. So instead of pursuing an entire degree in this field (which would take a few years) or starting my own organic farm on a large scale (which would take some money and entails a bit of a learning curve), I could instead travel somewhere else and stay on an organic farm. It's a win-win-win situation. I don't have to invest my time and resources into something I may or may not end up liking, plus I get a free place to stay! When you choose one of the varied helper opportunities, you'll be able to dip your toes into an experience that may not be available to you otherwise.

Personally, I'm keeping my eyes peeled for farm work in a little town near the ocean, or even a business internship for a hotel or touristic business to help increase the number of visitors and revenues in exchange for a bed and some food. It'd be a great way to help a family and entrepreneurs boost their businesses and stimulate the local economy. The great thing about HelpX and WorkAway is that they both offer opportunities that don't seem like 'work' but rather as fun, cool opportunities that make the time fly. Sort through this list and head to their websites; which opportunities catch your eye most? Pursue those experiences.

- **Accommodation businesses.** From luxurious eco-hotels that sit on the water to small, 'mom and pops' hotels in an urban city center, there are a plethora of accomodation opportunities available. Some of the most common options include working at a hostel, where you're usually expected to work in reception and clean, and maybe even organize fun outings like tours, pub crawls and more.
- **Language tutor.** If you're a native English speaker, you've got plenty of opportunities to choose from. You can choose to become a volunteer teacher in a rural school tucked in the mountains in Nepal or simply live with a family looking to teach their young children how to speak English (or any other language). Not a native English speaker? No problem (in most cases). Since this is on a voluntary basis, the requirements aren't as high as they are for paid English teachers.
- **Farmwork.** Just like the opportunities you can find on WWOOF, you'll find plenty of opportunities to work on mostly organic farms on both HelpX and Workaway. If your idea of paradise is breaking a sweat, working hard and unplugging from the buzz of the modern world, working on a farm is for you. You'll find farm opportunities in virtually every corner of the world.
- **Yachting and sailing.** If you didn't know, boating takes a lot of work. You'll be able to help out with small business owners who offer boat chartering services to vacationers and the elite and you may even find an opportunity to volunteer as a skipper or deckhand (though these options are usually paid - and they usually pay well!). If being out at sea appeals to you and you

want to spend the summer relaxing on the beach, connecting with boat owners can be your golden ticket to do so.

- **Veterinary services and animal shelters.** If you've got a heart for helping animals, there's a place for you as a Helper. Many organizations are opening their doors and their homes to volunteers like you in exchange for help spaying and neutering street dogs and cats. You'll also find unique opportunities caring for exotic wildlife - everything from frogs to monkeys - in Central and South America. If you want to help others help animals, this option is for you. And who knows - you may even decide to become a veterinarian at the end of your experience or become the next Jane Goodall.
- **Sustainability projects.** So many people are living greener, more sustainable lifestyles to help combat things like pollution (of both our air and water) and reduce the use of non-renewable sources of energy and single-use plastics. This category is a bit of a mixed bag. You'll find organic farming opportunities, stay with families and communities in off-grid communities and help with local sustainability non-profits.
- **Au Pairing and nannying.** Do you love kids? Are you patient and willing to help single moms or busy, working parents with childcare? If so, you might be the right candidate for Au Pairing programs. As I mentioned before this is almost exclusively limited to females. Though, if the family in need of an Au Pair has all male children and are open minded, I've also seen some families open to having a male nanny. If you're hesitant to participate in travel exchange programs, this option is great for a first-timer since you'll have a family to support you.
- **Non-profit organizations.** There are so many different types of non-profits to choose from including wildlife conservation organizations, help with refugees, helping in inner-cities and urban environments and more. If you're passionate about

helping people, animals and the planet, you'll be able to find the right opportunity that allows you to pair travel with your volunteerism.

- **Communities.** There are groups of people scattered round the world who reject modern living. Whether out of environmental reasons or to escape looming governments and Big Brother, or simply to be part of a right-knit community, there are many reasons to join a commune. If the idea of working a few hours each week to help make the community run (whether that's farming, chopping wood, sewing, etc.) appeals to you, you'll find many suitable communities on HelpX and Workaway.
- **Cultural exchanges.** This option is arguably the easiest of all: all you need to be is yourself! Many families and individuals are simply interested in bringing in people from around the world to exchange culture, languages and viewpoints. If this is something that interests you, you may luck out and find a family who wants to expose their children to different views and ways of lives or an individual who wants to pick your brain on your culture.

As you can see, there are so many Helper opportunities (and many others that I haven't even mentioned). Once you visit HelpX or Workaway, you'll be blown away by how many people are a part of this travel experience. Since I've used both HelpX and Workaway, I wanted to go over both platforms to help you decide which one to use since they do cost some money - but nothing compared to what you'd pay in accomodation! Here's my weigh-in on HelpX.net and Workaway.info. Find out which is right for you.

A Comparison of HelpX.net and Workaway.info

Signing up is simple on both of the sites. All it takes is you to fill in the required information and process the payment. Workaway.info is priced at roughly $30 for just one year, while Helpx.net is only $20 for two years. They both have their pros and cons. One thing I have learned is that it's important to apply well in advance. This is true for both HelpX and also Workaway. At the very least, you should apply one month ahead, and in some cases, up to 6 months before. Spaces can fill in pretty quickly, so be sure you get in there early. For example, even if it's only approaching March, if you're looking for a summer position it'd be best to look now. As you will see, the helper options are flexible and are mostly centered around providing language skills and helping around the house or a business. While working just 20 to 25 hours a week with a flexible schedule, it's a great way to see the world while helping out families and organizations; all at no charge to you.

Workaway.info

Workaway.info is often the first stop for many international volunteers. Not only do they have a website you can browse on your computer, there's also a convenient app, too. Workaway is much more sophisticated in its design and is incredibly user friendly compared to HelpX.net. You can browse tons of photos, see reviews left by other travelers in guest profiles and narrow down your search by a variety of search parameters (e.g. the type of work, location, etc.). On top of that, there are over 40,000 hosts, making Workaway.info the largest resource for independently organized helper exchanges.

What Workaway.info Is Best At:

- **User-friendly.** Workaway.info is so user-friendly that it's not just young people that use the platform. When you look at the Workaway program ambassadors, you'll see there are plenty of volunteers who are a bit older! Why? The website is clean and easy to use.
- **Convenient App for Phone.** Instead of hopping on your laptop, you can browse and save potential opportunities on

your phone, making it easier to connect to your next Workway experience.

- **Slightly More Popular Than HelpX.net.** WorkAway is home to more than 40,000 hosts - that's a lot of opportunity for you to take advantage of! Since there are so many hosts eagerly looking for helpers like you, this will greatly increase the chances you're chosen for a help exchange.
- **Better Developed Than HelpX.net.** As I'll cover below, HelpX isn't designed well. It does the job, but it doesn't look too pretty. It was first created in 2001 and looks like it, whereas Workaway.info has a more modern feel to the website, making it appear more active.

HelpX.net

HelpX is much more simplistic, on the other hand. The site could use a major face lift and it is a bit harder to navigate and narrow down your results. However, it definitely does the trick and hundreds of thousands of people have found volunteer exchanges using HelpX.net. Additionally, HelpX.net is larger and much more popular than workaway.info, not to mention the smaller price tag. I, myself, have never paid for Workaway.info and used HelpX.net. To me, it seems like many hosts post on both platforms, so you get more bang for your buck with HelpX.net. Plus, the membership is valid for two years instead one one.

What HelpX.net Is Best For You If:

- **You Want to Save Money.** Since HelpX.net only costs $20 and lasts for 2 years, you'll save a substantial amount if you choose to use this platform. However, since it's dated, you may pay for it in other ways i.e. some hosts may prefer Workaway over HelpX and not find your profile.

- **You're Hoping to Stand Out.** It seems that HelpX has a smaller pool of applicants which makes it easier for yours to shine when writing hosts. Less users means less competition.
- **You're Planning on Traveling Longer.** Since the membership is for two years and not one, you'll be able to travel longer and utilize this platform. Workaway, on the other hand, only has a one year membership.
- **You Don't Mind a Dated Design.** Once you type in HelpX.net in your browser, you'll see what I mean. The website isn't very eye-catching or clean, but it still gets the job done.

No matter which platform you choose, I hope you find an opportunity (or several!) that fulfills both your desire to help others and travel the world for free. Help exchanges are a great way to get to know people around the world, develop new skills and help regular people who could use a helping hand - even if they're not a part of a government-sponsored program. If you want to become part of the family abroad and make a difference, sign up for HelpX or Workaway now!

How to Start Your Journey Helping Around the World Now

1. Sign up on either HelpX or Workaway. After reading through the pros and cons of each platform and visiting both of them yourself, pick the one that you think will be most useful.
2. Find multiple opportunities that interest you. Find at least a couple to up to ten opportunities that interest you. Save them and be sure to apply. Describe why you'd be the best candidate and ensure you meet their requirement (e.g. some hosts require you stay for a minimum of one month, etc.)
3. Fill out your profile completely. Let hosts get to know you as a person. What are your hobbies and interests, what kinds of

foods do you eat, what do you value? But, also convey that you're reliable and hard-working.

4. Plan in advance. Be sure to research and start applying to volunteer positions a few months out. This is especially important if you're looking for a summer volunteer exchange - they fill quickly!
5. Ask your host questions and coordinate everything before you leave. You want to make sure your accommodation arrangements and working hours are agreed upon before you leave.

AmeriCorps (NCC, VISTA, State, National and Senior Corps)

Skills Needed	Being physically fit is a huge plus as some of the programs may be physically demanding (particularly AmeriCorps NCCC). Additionally, must have professional skills if working in an office environment.
Hours Per Week	AmeriCorps is full-time (roughly 40 hours per week) for 10 months to a year. Select summer programs are available for 3 months or less.
Requirements and Restrictions	Must be 17+. Limited to ages 18-26 for AmeriCorps NCCC (although there are opportunities for those to lead groups who are older than 24) and must have a high school diploma. For the VISTA and State and National program, there is no upper age limit (for State

	and Senior, the minimum age is 17). Additionally, there is also a Senior Corps program for those who are a bit older and have some wisdom and expertise to lend.
Location	All over the US. From urban settings to rural countryside.

If you've ever volunteered anywhere, chances are you've heard of the AmeriCorps program. My first interaction with the AmeriCorps program was when I was 16 years old and scored an internship at a non-profit in Bellingham called Animals as Natural Therapy. There were two ladies there called "Vistas" meaning they were a part of the AmeriCorps VISTA program. They were passionate and dedicated to help others; it was very clear they chose this path not for the money (you do get a stipend, but it's very modest) but to help others. After seeing their impact they had on the organization and the people they helped, it inspired me to one day take part in the program too. To give you a quick introduction to AmeriCorps, it's a program (like the Peace Corps, which is even more well-known) that allows primarily young adults to give back to local communities - either in their own hometown or somewhere else new and exciting. If you grew up in a small town and want to help elementary school students in the big city, for example, AmeriCorps can help you do that. That way you'll be able to live your dream of living in a big city while sharing your passion of teaching children and being a positive role model. It works on the flip-side too: if you grew up in the city and have always wanted to help on a farm or run outdoor wildlife retreats for kids, AmeriCorps gives you that chance! As of now in 2020, there are 75,000 members serving in 21,000 locations within the USA and over one million alumni. Needless to say the program is very popular - and for good reason! If you're looking for a unique gap year program or aren't quite sure of what career you'd like to pursue, don't sleep on the opportunity to join AmeriCorps!

Looking back, if I were to stay in the US and didn't go off to get my degree in Business and Management in Italy I would have chosen to apply to AmeriCorps programs! AmeriCorps provides life changing experiences for thousands of American citizens each year who would like to make a difference in their country. AmeriCorps volunteers are placed in non-profit organizations, schools, public agencies as well as community groups throughout the country where they work long hours (full-time) out of sheer passion and service. If you're up for the challenge and are willing to put in full-time hours towards a program you're passionate about, apply to AmeriCorps. The best part of AmeriCorps is that you can choose from a variety of organizations that are in line with what you'd like to do in the future. For example, if you think you want to become a teacher, rather than go straight to school for it, it may be smart to tutor kids first with AmericCorps to ensure that is something you like to do and are good at. Don't be intimidated if you're still applying as a senior high school student or have recently graduated. In fact, AmeriCorps makes a great "gap year" program as you transition from high school and university (plus, many of the programs offer a stipend that can be used towards your education!)

What Type of AmeriCorps Volunteer Will You Be?

AmeriCorps is a blanket term for its four departments: AmeriCorps NCCC; AmeriCorps Vista; AmeriCorps State and National, and Senior Corps. In the following sections, I'll go over how they differ, what you can expect from each of the programs, and each of their requirements.

1. **AmeriCorps NCCC.** If you want to explore the United Statesand live with a supportive, tight-knit team, AmeriCorps

NCCC may be right for you. This branch of AmeriCorps breaks into two sub-branches: Traditional Corps and FEMA Corps. Traditional Corps is for hands-on projects like environmental conservation and urban development i.e. construction, while FEMA Corps is more administrative and helps the nation prepare and cope with disaster.

2. **AmeriCorps VISTA.** This program, created in 1965, is focused on "lifting people out of poverty." VISTA stands for Volunteers in Service to America and helps local communities eradicate poverty and social inequality on a local level. There are three roles part of the VISTA program: being a Member, Leader and Summer Associate.
3. **AmeriCorps State and National.** This portion of AmeriCorps is the largest. You'll have far more opportunities available through AmeriCorps State and National as a volunteer. Additionally, the minimum age is only 17, perfect for those who have graduated a semester early or who want to volunteer on a part-time basis. The hours aren't as set in stone as they are for the former two branches of AmeriCorps; rather, you will choose programs that have an allotted number of hours you must commit to.
4. **Senior Corps.** If you're older or retired, there are a few programs within the Senior Corps that help relieve loneliness among other seniors, fill the role as a grandparent for youth, and help recover from disaster. Those who help in the Senior Corps (there are 200,000+ volunteers each year with over 50,000,000 hours served each year!) report being healthier and happier due to their volunteerism.

AmeriCorps NCCC

If you don't mind putting in a bit of sweat equity to benefit the greater good and can remain calm during crises, joining AmeriCorps NCCC would be an ideal option for you. But first, what does NCCC mean? NCCC stands for National Civilian Community Corps. As previously mentioned, there are two sub-branches within NCCC which I'll explain below. AmeriCorps NCCC is a great option for anybody over the ages 18-24 who is interested in building and restoring communities, and helping prevent and mitigate disasters. One thing that makes NCCC stand out is that you are assigned to a home base in the US, from which you will have various "missions" that allow you the possibility to travel within the region. Another huge bonus: you're provided with accomodation (unlike the other programs which provide you a stipend that should cover rent, but leave it to you to sort out your accommodation).

The regions you can serve in within the US include:

- Denver, Colorado
- Sacramento, California
- Baltimore, Maryland
- Vicksburg, Mississippi
- Vinton, Iowa

Note that the above locations serve as home bases, but you will likely have the opportunity to travel within the region. For example, a friend of mine who participated in AmeriCorps NCCC in the Baltimore, Maryland program was able to come visit me in New York City since her team was located nearby for a project. As part of the AmeriCorps NCCC program, you receive free housing and food during the entirety of your 10 month term. Not only do you get free room and board, you also earn a living allowance (which is around $400 each month). According to the official AmeriCorps NCCC website: "When you are not serving on a regional campus, you can expect to stay in various forms of lodging accommodations such as community centers, churches, campgrounds, or motel/hotel rooms. [They] will pay for your travel expenses to your regional campus. When you are not on campus, [they] will provide full travel accommodations for you to serve at your team's assigned locations. You can expect to travel in 15-passenger vans that are provided by our program." It's a win-win situation: you are making money while having the opportunity to travel regionally, with room and board fully included. Sure, it may not be as exotic as helping in an orphanage in Bali, but the truth is there are plenty of beautiful, natural places in the US and AmeriCorps NCCC can help you get your foot in the door for future employment - including in the government.

Throughout the program you are allotted a $4,000 living allowance and will receive at least $5,775 (taxable) as an educational award upon completion of the program. The educational award can be applied toward future studies at a university or college and can even be used retroactively to pay qualified student loans. If you're still undecided about going into college and want to travel the world, this is not a bad deal!

FEMA Corps vs. Traditional Corps

As mentioned, there are two divisions: FEMA Corps (which focuses on relieving disasters) and the Traditional Corps. Both programs are similar in that they offer a Segal AmeriCorps Education Award, full room and board, travel opportunities and a stipend, but here's where they start to divide. FEMA Corps is much more "behind the scenes" i.e. you won;t be working with your hands so much removing invasive plant species, restoring parks and building community centers as you would with the Traditional Corps. Instead, you'll be working directly with people affected by disaster and connecting them to qualified disaster-relief organizations, sorting out how to get from Point A to Point B i.e. logistics, and will be tasked with collecting valuable data post natural disaster. In summary, FEMA is much more humanistic and disaster-focused. If you value working closely with others and are the type of person to stand up and lead during periods of crisis, this program is for you.

Traditional Corps, on the other hand is more project-based and helps people in an indirect way by developing valuable infrastructure and creating sustainable green spaces. If you're not a "people person" and like working with your hands, Traditional Corps is likely a good fit. According to their website, "As a Traditional Corps member, you and your team will serve on at least four different projects in different states and cities within your assigned region of the country. Projects are designed to address one or more of these issue areas: Energy Conservation, Environmental Stewardship, Infrastructure Improvement, Natural and Other Disasters, and Urban and Rural Development." As you can see, the Traditional Corps creates things for others to enjoy in an indirect way, while FEMA Corps works directly with affected individuals and crisis workers during natural and other disasters.

Team Member vs. Team Leader

Over 24? Unfortunately, if you want to be a team member of both Traditional Corps and FEMA Corps, you'll need to be between 18 and 24 years old. But if you're older, don't worry! You can still apply as a team leader for both branches of AmeriCorps NCCC as there is no upper age limit. The difference between being a team member and a team lead is you'll serve an additional month as a team leader and you receive an allowance that is much higher at $12,500 along with the $5,775 education award. It's a very similar experience, though it requires you to be a bit more responsible and act as the leader of your team, as the title suggests. If that's something you're up for, create a profile and sign up for one of the most moving experiences of your life! Visit nationalservice.gov to learn more about the programs and find the right role.

AmeriCorps VISTA

Next is the AmeriCorps VISTA division, which stands for Volunteers in Service to America. This portion of AmeriCorps selects 7,000 VISTA volunteers annually to help communities across America live better lives. The primary goal of this branch of AmeriCorps is to relieve families, individuals, and entire communities of poverty. AmeriCorps VISTA is open to all citizens or legal residents over the age of 18 (yes, even people over 24 years of age unlike the team member positions in AmeriCorps NCCC). Instead of working hands-on in the field of an organization and assisting participants of the programs directly, VISTA volunteers work within a project or organization's structure. If you decide to apply to the AmeriCorps VISTA program, you'll spend most of your time dealing with the administrative and financial aspects of the organization you're assigned to. Per the AmeriCorps VISTA page: "AmeriCorps VISTA members build capacity in nonprofit organizations and public agencies to help them more effectively generate the commitment of private sector resources, encourage volunteer service at the local level, and empower individuals and communities. AmeriCorps VISTA members serve full time for one-year terms." Unlike the AmeriCorps NCCC branch, you'll need to stick to the VISTA program for an entire year. That way you can leave a lasting impression in the communities you serve.

Here's what you can help with as an AmeriCorps VISTA volunteer:

- **Adult Literacy.** Develop and connect adults to literacy programs to improve their lives and society at large.
- **Inner City Youth Programs**. Work toward lowering crime and increasing graduation rates in America's most vulnerable urban centers.
- **Access to Healthcare.** Connect low income families to health insurance programs.

- **Combat Homelessness.** Coordinate transitional housing for the homeless population with support to help them overcome financial, mental health and drug-related issues.
- **And More!** There are tons of other unique services that benefit American citizens all over the country. Find the right opportunity for you www.nationalservice.gov.

VISTA volunteers are the men and women in the background that don't get as recognized and praised as often as they should for helping the US population. If you want to become an unsung hero, consider joining the VISTA program. You'll be able to develop your professional skills like budgeting, marketing and strategic planning that can translate directly into your future career. Since the VISTA program is so wide-spread and there are so many positions available throughout the US, you will be able to relocate to practically anywhere. From the urban center or Chicago to a rural town in the Rocky mountains - you may even end up in Bellingham, Washington! Now, let's talk about compensation and stipend (a huge benefit of this program). No, you won't be making a fortune. In fact, your greatest payment will come from knowing that you're helping vulnerable, struggling populations and bettering the lives of others. But, on the brightside, the monthly alloted stipend should cover your expenses and you'll be able to live life as far away - or as near - from home as you'd like. Volunteers work countless hours and are given just enough money to live a basic lifestyle. Don't expect to be going out for a night on the town often, to be able to afford fancy, designer clothes and live lavishly; you're provided with just enough to cover food and rent. You will earn a small modest living allowance, and if you are serving for a year you'll have access to some healthcare benefits, childcare services, and Federal Non-Competitive (NCE) hiring eligibility, among other benefits. Upon completion you are also entitled to receive a post-service stipend. This stipend can either be in cash or as a much larger educational

educational award. Of course, money isn't the focus of most volunteers, but the cash or education stipend is a bonus that can be added to your savings account or college fund. Basically, you're getting paid to live in an exciting, new US destination while helping others. It doesn't get any better than that!

The VISTA program is the option that I would have chosen had I not gone off to pursue my Business and Management degree in Italy. Not only does the VISTA program put your foot in the door for future jobs (including government-level jobs), but it's a feel-good program that helps you feel a part of something larger than yourself. One of the main benefits is that as a VISTA volunteer, you're given the opportunity to manage and lead an organization - not just bring coffees and fill in data entry forms. That way once the year is over, you'll have plenty of accomplishments to talk about in future interviews and your LinkedIn will be sure to shine. Another great thing is that there are three different roles (with one, the Summer Associate position, allowing you to be a part of the program for just a couple of months if you're hesitant to commit for an entire year).

The Three Roles Within Americorps VISTA

- **Member.** To be a member, you must be 18 years old or older. No experience is required - perfect for high school graduates looking to build their resume. You can serve anywhere in the US and will be given a monthly living allowance to cover your expenses. At the end of the 12 months, you'll be given two options: 1. A $6,195 education award or 2. A $1,800 cash stipend.
- **Leader.** You must be 18 years or older and differ from the "Member" role: you must have had at least one year of full-time service in AmeriCorps or Peace Corps. On top of the determined living allowance, you'll get $200 extra each month.

At the end of the 12 months, you'll be given two options: 1. A $6,195 education award or 2. A $3,000 cash stipend.

- **Summer Associate.** Unlike the other two roles, when you're a VISTA summer associate, you only serve for 8, 9, or 10 weeks rather than a full year. As such, your stipend is smaller at the end of the program ($1,311 as an education award or a cash stipend between $276 and $345. Like the other options, your monthly allowance depends on the cost of living in the location you decide to serve in.

AmeriCorps State and National

And the last sector of the AmeriCorps foundation is the State and National which is less defined than the other options in the sense that it's not disaster-specific or poverty alleviation-specific. If you can think of a way to help others and the planet, there's probably a program you can become a part of through AmeriCorps State and National. When you visit the AmeriCorps website, you'll find that you can, "Find the AmeriCorps State and National program that fits you; search hundreds of opportunities, choose a part- or full-time program, select your interest area, and earn a Segal AmeriCorps Education Award." As you can see, there are a few things that make AmeriCorps State and National a bit different from the other branches of AmeriCorps. While you'll be eligible for an educational reward (Segal AmeriCorps Education Award) and will receive a monthly stipend to help you cover room and board you aren't required to join an organization for an entire year and can even work part-time (whereas NCCC and VISTA are full-time). Additionally, the minimum age for the State and National program is only 17, meaning you'll be able to take on a full or part-time position as a high school student. Plus, if you're not interested in working in an office as you would as a VISTA and aren't interested in disaster relief and construction work - that's fine! There are plenty of other areas that will likely fulfill your unique skills and interests.

AmeriCorps State and National primarily focuses on the following areas:

- Community and Nonprofit Development
- Disaster Services
- Economic and Workforce Development
- Education
- Energy and Conservation
- Health and Nutrition
- Legal Assistance
- Tribes and Native American Affairs
- Veterans and Military Families
- Youth Development and Mentoring

As you can see there are opportunities for almost everyone - not just for those interested in managing non-profits and preventing and alleviating disaster-stricken people. If, for example, you're thinking about going to medical school, you may be able to volunteer in a clinic first to see if that's really how you want to spend the rest of your working life. Or, if you're thinking of becoming a social worker, you may decide to work with a foster home, adoption agency or at a domestic violence shelter. There are thousands of opportunities for you to choose from. And since there is no set start time (as there is with the NCCC program) you'll be able to apply to volunteer positions with State and National throughout the year. To get started, head to nationalservice.gov and create a profile - you'll be able to access all kinds of interesting opportunities all over the US!

Senior Corps

Before we dig into Senior Corps, I just want to clarify something about the previous branches of AmeriCorps: there's no upper age limit for any of the programs except for AmeriCorps NCCC (and eve then you can still participate, but only as a team leader and not as a member). What is the Senior Corps? According to the official website, "Senior Corps is a network of national service programs for Americans 55 years and older, made up of three primary programs that each take a different approach to improving lives and fostering civic engagement. Senior Corps volunteers commit their time to address critical community needs including academic tutoring and mentoring, elderly care, disaster relief support, and more." Basically, Senior Corps is for adults aged 55 and older and has three sub-branches, which are:

- **Foster Grandparents.** When you become a foster grandparent, you're helping add some normalcy to a child's life. Whether a child doesn't have grandparents in their life because of divorce, addiction problems, or death, you'll be able to fill that role in a meaningful way. You can help children by being their mentor, friend and tutor. If this interests you, click on the "Senior Corps" page on www.nationalservice.gov.
- **RSVP.** Join one of the largest organizations for seniors over 55 years old in a variety of projects and organizations. You'll be able to put your skills to use to organize neighborhood watch programs, tutor and mentor disadvantaged and disabled youth, renovate homes, teach English to immigrants and assist in times of disaster. With this program, unlike Foster Grandparents and Senior Companions (which offer modest monthly stipends) there is no monetary gain.
- **Seniors Companions.** Loneliness and addiction are more common than you'd think among other seniors. Some simply need help with daily tasks in their home. If you want to help other seniors remain independent in their own homes, this program is for you.

Want to Participate in AmeriCorps? Here's How to Take Action:

1. Determine which branch you'd like to be a part of (NCC, VISTA, State and National)
2. Make sure you meet all of the minimum requirements (i.e. age, citizen and/or permanent residency status, etc.) before you apply.
3. Visit www.nationalservice.gov and sort through the available opportunities. Select the opportunities that appeal to you most. You can base this decision on their location or the type of organization.
4. Apply to the selected opportunities. You'll need to fill out applications for each of the opportunities you want to apply to (which aren't too time consuming). Don't put it off; if you want to travel the world and make a difference, it's important you fill your application out promptly and completely.
5. Become an attractive candidate. What are you doing now to prepare yourself to help others? For example, if you're planning on applying to a VISTA opportunity in an office, you may consider getting a Microsoft certificate to boost your candidacy. Or, you may download Duolingo to learn another language. Be productive and pursue the best version of yourself.

The Peace Corps

Skills Needed	Since the areas the Peace Corps focuses on are education, agriculture, community economic development, health, environment and youth, it's best if you have experience and compassion working in these fields.
Hours Per Week	If you're chosen for the Peace Corps you must commit to 2 years plus 3 months of training prior to departure. Expect to work full-time during your experience.
Requirements and Restrictions	Must be 18 years or older. Additionally, you're almost always required to have a Bachelor's degree since the program was designed for students to gain real-world experience. You'll also need to be comfortable living in conditions you're unused to (e.g. sleeping in a mud hut, using a communal latrine, having to walk 20

	minutes for water, etc.) Some programs require proficiency in languages.
Location	Africa (almost half of Peace Corp volunteers are assigned to Africa), Asia, Eastern Europe and Central Asia, and Latin America.

When kids grow up, they dream of being police officers, firefighters, astronauts, teachers, models or even the President of the United States. But not me - I wanted to be a lawyer (I have no idea why) and also wanted to join the Peace Corps. If you're like me i.e. passionate about traveling and helping others, the Peace Corps is the perfect way to merge those two together. What I like most about the Peace Corps is you're expected to live like a local. You won't be given a higher living standard, rather you'll have to rough it in mud huts in a small village in Africa for example, just like the local population. I imagine this would be a transformative, life-changing experience which attracts me and so many others. The Peace Corps throws you out of your comfort zone and norms and places you in a society completely different from your own. A bit on the history of the Peace Corps: it was created via an Executive Order by President John F. Kennedy in 1962. Since then, more than 235,000 US citizens have participated in the program. The application process is quite long, requiring that you apply 9-12 months in advance, so if you want to join the program be sure to take proactive steps now. Whether you choose an opportunity that helps with education, healthcare, or business, you will make a difference in the world in others' lives as a Peace Corps volunteer. Not only will you create real, long-lasting change for others, you'll also foster change within yourself in a profound way, too.

Where Can You Serve as a Peace Corps Volunteer?

If you have a college degree and want to serve around the world,there are plenty of interesting destinations to choose from! Currently, there are volunteers placed all over the world, including:

- **Africa.** Sub-Saharan Africa makes up the largest areas served with around 45% of volunteers placed in Southern and Central Africa. There are an additional 3% of volunteers in Northern Africa (Tunisia and Morocco).
- **The Americas.** As for the Americas, 26% of volunteers are located in Latin America with nearly half in Central America in countries (Belize, El Salvador, Costa Rica, Nicaragua, Panama and Costa Rica) and Mexico. If you want to head even more south, South America is also an option. Volunteers are scattered in South Africa to a lesser extent.
- **Asia.** If you want to go to Asia, there is certainly room for you there with 12% of volunteers being placed in Central and Southern Asian countries, such as China, Indonesia, Mongolia, Thailand and Nepal.
- **Europe.** The remaining 10% serve in Eastern European countries (Kosovo, Albania and Macedonia) as well as Central Asian countries that border Europe like Armenia, Kyrgyzstan and Georgia.

Those are some pretty interesting locations, right? If you want to live like a local for two years of your life and instill lasting beneficial changes, sign up to the Peace Corps now. One thing to note: I'm sure some countries capture your attention more than others. You may want to feel the African sun beating strongly on your back, or breather in the unspoiled air in the secluded Caucasus Mountains. But unfortunately you aren't able to choose where the Peace Corps places you. However, you do have a slight say (i.e. you can identify your preferred locations and programs) and can choose from the various open positions around the world. One thing you can do to boost your chances of being selected for your top pick location is to start preparing now. Want to go to China? Start learning Chinese now with your favorite application. Write blog posts on the history of China. Look up recipes on authentic Chinese food. Try to start immersing yourself in the culture and language now to express your strong interest in a particular place; don't leave it to chance.

How Peace Corps Volunteers Make a Difference

Before you actually apply, you may be wondering what it is you do exactly as a Peace Corps volunteer. Volunteers are split into six sectors (I've also included a description from www.peacecorps.gov to give you an idea of what you'd be doing in each sector):

1. **Education.** "Volunteers play an important role in creating links among schools, parents, and communities. They may work in elementary, secondary, or post secondary schools, teaching subjects such as math, science, or conversational English; or as resource teachers or teacher trainers. Volunteers also develop libraries and technology resource centers."
2. **Agriculture.** "Agriculture Volunteers work with small-scale farmers and families to increase food security and production and adapt to climate change while promoting environmental conservation."
3. **Community Economic Development.** "Volunteers work with development banks, nongovernmental organizations, and municipalities to encourage economic opportunities in communities. They frequently teach in classroom settings and work with entrepreneurs and business owners to develop and market their products."

4. **Health.** "Health Volunteers work within their communities to promote important topics such as nutrition, maternal and child health, basic hygiene, and water sanitation."
5. **Environment.** "Volunteers lead grassroots efforts to protect the environment and strengthen understanding of environmental issues. They teach environmental awareness in schools and to local organizations, empowering communities to make their own decisions about how to conserve the local environment."
6. **Youth In Development.** "Volunteers work with youth in communities to promote engagement and active citizenship, including gender awareness, employability, health and HIV/AIDS education, environmental awareness, sports and fitness programs, and information technology."

There's something for everyone. If you've earned your degree and want to put the theory you've learned in practice, the Peace Corps proved an excellent opportunity to do so. What you do can vary day by day; you may be working in a clinic (if you have the required degree and certifications) where you see the local people. Other times, you may have to travel to a neighboring town to help someone who is sick. For community economic development, for example, you will be tasked with teaching others how to become financially literate, acting as a consultant for local businesses. You could even be a positive role model for kids and teach them English via fun activities. It's all varied and is sure to be a rewarding experience for both you and the population you serve.

Some Things to Consider Before You Join the PeaceCorps

The Peace Corps isn't something you can just "wing". The application process is fairly competitive and takes around a year to complete. You have to be sure you can fully commit; that means blocking out your schedule for two years and three months. Can you do that? Here are four things to think about before you click "APPLY" on www.peacecorps.gov:

1. **You Can't Choose Your Location.** As mentioned, you don't have the final say in the location you're chosen for. That being said, you can always boost your chance by pursuing skills specifically for that assignment.
2. **You'll Need to Start the Application a Year In Advance.** With the Peace Corps, you can't just apply a couple weeks or months in advance. It's best to start the process a year ahead. Be sure to factor in that time, as well as the three months of training required before starting your experience abroad.
3. **The Duration Is 2 Years. Can You Commit to That?** That means two years without seeing your family and friends. Two years living in a different culture, adopting a different lifestyle. It can be hard for some, but it's sure to be completely life-changing. Just be sure you can stick it out for the entire duration.
4. **Life Abroad May Not Be What You're Used To.** If you're the type of person that needs to wake up with a cup of coffee from your favorite cafe and can't live without your car, you probably won't do well with the Peace Corps. You need to be adaptive and flexible; that often means giving up your modern luxuries.

If you think you have what it takes, visit the Peace Corps website to learn more and apply. On top of the obvious benefit of being able to travel and live like a local somewhere else in the world, there are plenty other benefits to joining the Peace Corps. One of the greatest benefits is the name factor; people read "Peace Corps" and instantly assume you're a well-traveled, cultured and generous person. Additionally, you'll have preferential status when applying for jobs in the government. In terms of a stipend and financial rewards, you'll be provided with a monthly allowance as well as two paid days off per month (which you can use to explore the surrounding area). At the end of the successfully completed program, you'll also be awarded $10,000 to help you ease back into life in the US. Clearly, the biggest reward has little to do with money; volunteers use the Peace Corps to develop their professional skills, help others and travel in an authentic way. If this appeals to you, don't put off your application- start now!

How to Take Action Now

1. Ensure you meet all requirements. The Peace Corps requires that you be at least 18 years old and possess a Bachelor's degree.
2. Explore the open positions on www.peacecorps.gov. Save a few that interest you most and are in-line with your skills and what you've studied in university.
3. Develop skills and language capabilities now. Try to take a few weeks to get certified in things you think would boost your candidacy. For example, if you are working with kids, you may consider getting a degree in CPR for safety. If working in economic development, you may consider getting a Google certificate.
4. Complete the application. You'll need to include important things like your resume and motivation for serving a letter (which should be around 500 words), three references and certificates for foreign language skills.
5. Connect with a recruiter. This isn't required, but according to the Peace Corps website, "Applicants who connect with a recruiter are 55% more likely to become Volunteers." If you want to boost your candidacy, this is a must; 55% more likely is significant! If transportation is an issue and there's nobody

nearby, see if you can schedule a Skype call. The bottom line is it important to express your interest to someone in the organization and become a real person rather than a bunch of words on paper.

The Ultimate Volunteer Exchange Resource List

I've compiled a list of free (or near-free) programs that can help you see the world at little to no cost. There are so many volunteer programs out there that charge hundreds - or even thousands - of dollars each week just to volunteer. While I understand organizations have costs, it shouldn't fall on the shoulders of the volunteers. That's why I found these opportunities that allow you to help in exchange for free accommodation.

US-based Volunteer Programs

Who says you need to leave the country for an authentic volunteer experience? If you're apprehensive about crossing borders for the first time and want to stay in the US, the following opportunities are great for you - especially if you're looking for a Gap Year experience.

- **International Volunteer Exchange Program (IVEP).** This opportunity is for Christian adults to volunteer throughout the US and Canada. IVEP is, "a yearlong volunteer work and cultural exchange opportunity for young, Christian adults. Every year 60 IVEP participants come from more than 25 countries around the world to volunteer in the U.S. or Canada, where they live with a local person or family. Since its beginning in 1950, IVEP has emphasized peacemaking and building understanding across cultures." More information at mcc.org.

- **City Year.** If you want to be a positive role-model for kids for 11 months in high-need areas of the US, this opportunity is for you. "As a City Year AmeriCorps member, you'll work long days within a complex school system with many partners and stakeholders. You will manage relationships and expectations with teammates, school staff, partner teachers, students, families and the school district." See cityyear.org for more information on accommodation, stipend and other important details.
- **Seney National Wildlife Refuge.** "Each year the Seney National Wildlife Refuge searches for one to three residential volunteers. These volunteers are invited to lodge on the refuge, free of charge, in their camper or recreational vehicle for a few weeks or a few months. In turn, the volunteers are required to work 20 to 40 hours per week for the duration of their stay." See https://www.fws.gov/refuge/seney/jobs/volunteer.html for more.
- **Forest Animal Rescue.** "We have a program where volunteers from the US and abroad can pay in advance for their housing and food, then stay in our housing and volunteer with us full time. This is the best way to truly learn about the operation of the sanctuary and build your resume." Visit https://www.forestanimalrescue.org/ to apply.

Programs Similar to the Peace Corps

Since the Peace Corps is so popular, there's a chance your application may not be accepted. If that's the case or you want to play your cards safe, you can always opt for one of the following options. Plus, these programs have shorter required stays making it easier to commit.

- **United Nations Volunteers.** "International UN Volunteers promote peace and development in communities around the globe, while upholding the ideals and aspirations of the United Nations… As an international UN Volunteer, you will learn about different cultures, expand your networks, study foreign languages and gain matchless professional and life experiences."www.unv.org/
- **Servas.** "Servas provides opportunities for personal connections among people of diverse cultures toward the goal of promoting world peace, goodwill and understanding. Servas is a peacebuilding family with over 15,000 members in over 120 countries. We all united by the goal of breaking down cultural barriers and building peace. Through local community events, gatherings and projects, members of Servas are not just travelers and hosts but are the building blocks of an international movement begun in 1949 in post-war Europe." https://usservas.org/
- **Voluntary Service Overseas (VSO).** "VSO volunteers and partners reached over 1,000,000 people last year. They brought inspiration, energy and vital practical skills to help achieve community goals: better healthcare, more valuable education and broader opportunities." See www.vsointernational.org for more details.
- **Friends of Waldorf Education (Germany).** "Since 1993 the organisation Friends of Waldorf Education has been offering a variety of volunteering and community services worldwide, in Germany, and for people living abroad in Germany (Incoming)." Visit www.freunde-waldorf.de/en/ to explore this opportunity further.

- **Rural Organization for Social Elevation (ROSE).** Explore the Himalayan foothills and make a lasting impression on this Indian village in Uttarakhand, India. "R.O.S.E. (Rural Organization for Social Elevation) was founded in 1988 by Jeevan Verma after he became interested in social work to help his community. R.O.S.E. runs a public school for poorer families, has built 5 houses, a dozen composting toilets and helps with improving life in the valley in large and small ways." See www.volunteeringindiahimalayarosekanda.org.
- **Pyunli (India).** "Pyunli is looking for idealistic and competent people willing to give up some of their time to do something positive for the children of our community. You can teach english, yoga, music, dance, art & craft, origami etc based on your skills. Most of our volunteers have an amazing, life-enhancing experience. It is important to understand that Pyunli is not engaged in the 'voluntourism' business." https://pyunli.com/volunteer
- **Ladli (India).** If you have a heart for helping orphans gain valuable skills for the workforce, try out Ladli in Jaipur. "Volunteering with Ladli is simple. We do not charge any fees, nor do we pay any salary. You would be expected to make your own way to Jaipur and, although we can help arrange your accommodation, we do not pay for it. Once in Jaipur we would welcome you, bring you to Ladli, show you around and allow you to choose the kind of work you want to do. Volunteers typically work Monday-Friday 10am-5pm, but this is flexible." http://ladli.org/
- **Mandore Project (India).** "The project aims to organize fun, educational activities for rural school children in order to inspire them to learn and give them some much needed attention. You'll play games and sports, sing songs and do some arts-and-crafts, all aimed at teaching the kids basic English,

while giving them the attention and love they need and deserve. You might also expect to prepare and teach your own lessons as well, depending on the local need. You may also assist with some painting and renovation work as well." Visit www.mandoreproject.org/ to find out how you can help.

- **Seva Mandir (India).** "Seva Mandir's volunteer and internship programme provides an opportunity to gain an insight into the development sector through hands-on grass-roots work and to make a real contribution. We host over 150 volunteers and interns a year....Seva Mandir hosts volunteers and interns from leading academic institutions across India (for example, the Institute of Rural Management (IRMA), the Tata Institute of Social Sciences (TISS), the Institute of Chartered and Financial Analysist of India (ICFAI), the Indian Institute of Forrest Management (IIFM)) and from universities abroad (including Yale, Columbia, Duke, Oxford, Sussex and Edinburgh). We also receive volunteers and interns through programmes such as those at the National Foundation of India, Voluntary Service Overseas (VSO), America India Foundation and the Foundation for Sustainable Development. Seva Mandir is a partner with the State Bank of India (SBI) Youth for India Fellowship and India Fellow programmes." Does this sound like a good fit for you? Apply at www.sevamandir.org/
- **Paper Boat Charity (India).** "At the core of 'how we work' are child-centred creative learning spaces (called Children's Hubs) that equip young people with the skills, experience and personal qualities needed for creative problem solving and leading change in their communities. We work with local experts and grassroots community-based partners who help us to set up and run these hubs. Children's Hubs are community-owned spaces where children come to learn and play after school – helping to reinforce and extend what they

learn in school." Visit paperboatcharity.org.uk to find out how you can help.

- **Terre Des Homme Core (India).** "Our organization was created for rescuing children in need of care and protection, therefore we expect from our Volunteers a strong sensibility when spending their time with children and a keen interest in children rights. From International Volunteers, moreover, we expect adaptability and respect for our culture. We look for professionals who can bring an effective contribution to our projects and share their professional skills with our staff. The minimum age for volunteering with us is 25." See tdhcore.org to get involved.
- **Casa do Caminho (Brazil).** "Casa do Caminho is a Brazilian nonprofit organization with a philanthropic mission, which develops social, educational, cultural and sports projects, with the goal of helping poor families and children, and strengthening the bonds within rural communities in Brazil. The Volunteering Program offered by Casa do Caminho is completely free." See www.casadocaminhobrasil.org/ for more.
- **Sapa O'Chau (Vietnam).** "Sapa O'Chau provides high school age students accomodation so that they can attend high school in Sapa Town. This saves them from travelling more than 10 km a day mostly on foot to and from town and village. The ethnic minorities are not native speakers of Vietnamese language, hence they need extra coaching to catch up with their native Vietnamese-speaking counterparts. To support each youth costs Sapa O'Chau at least USD100 per month. This covers Vietnamese school fees, in-house tutoring to help catch up with peers, accommodation, utilities, food and personal hygiene supplies." Think you can make a difference? Visit http://sapaochau.org/.

Social Media Groups

If you're more adventurous and want to find an independently organized opportunity, you can always opt to scan through postings on social media. I've researched some of the best, most active groups (as of May, 2020) so that you can find a transformative travel experience through Facebook or Couchsurfing. Since there are so many groups (that can change or be deleted by the time you read this) I'll leave it to you to search for "Help Exchange," "International Volunteer," "Free Accomodation Volunteer" etc. to find the perfect travel volunteer experience for you.

Help Exchanges

I know I've already covered Workaway.info and HelpX.net, but if you're looking for some alternative resources, you can always try some of these programs. While they may not be as popular, they're either low-cost or completely free, so you have nothing to lose!

- **Hippo Help.** If you're looking for an easy to use - and best of all free - help exchange platform, try *hippohelp.com.* "Hippohelp is a free map-based work exchange platform connecting hosts from all over the world with travellers who are happy to work in exchange for free food and accommodation."
- **Worldpackers.** "Whether it's saving on your trip, immersing yourself in a local culture or developing new skills, you can use Worldpackers during your vacation time, backpacking trip or even taking a gap year. There are hostels, inns, NGOs, communities and ecological projects that you can help with and in exchange receive free stay, food and other benefits. There are more than one million travelers and hosts from 170 countries that are part of our community!" Visit *Worldpacker.com* for more information, or download their app!

- **HelpStay.com.** "HelpStay is a skills-based volunteering platform that connects travellers with Hosts of great projects around the world. Our platform makes travelling meaningful and affordable by allowing helpers to exchange work for accommodation. The host opportunities featured on our site have been vetted and reviewed by our staff, keeping our helpers safe and our community strong."
- **Volunteer Base.** "Volunteers Base is a moneyless help exchange network, it's free and always will be! Hosts in need of help list their Projects and Volunteers interested in joining can get in touch. Projects can be almost anything: farming, building, hostels, language teaching, house sitting, community work, arts and crafts, housekeeping, etc." Start your journey at *volunteersbase.com* now!
- **Kibbutz Volunteer.** If you're interested in sustainable farming, participating in kibbutz in Israel may be for you. "A kibbutz is a communal agricultural settlement in Israel, usually in a rural location. The "members" of the kibbutz are known as kibbutzniks. All property on the kibbutz is owned communally and all income generated is shared by the kibbutz." www.kibbutzvolunteer.com
- **Hospitality Club.** "The club is supported by volunteers who believe in one idea: by bringing travelers in touch with people in the place they visit, and by giving "locals" a chance to meet people from other cultures we can increase intercultural understanding and strengthen the peace on our planet." Visit hospitality.org for more details.
- **Anywork Anywhere.** Anywork Anywhere isn't just for paid opportunities abroad (though you can find paid positions in customer service, teaching languages, etc.), you can also find once in a lifetime volunteer opportunities, too. "AnyworkAnywhere.com is the English speaking department

from Working Adventures, an international recruitment agency that over the years has helped people land jobs in amazing destinations all around the world. AnyworkAnywhere.com offers the biggest selection of summer and winter jobs from some of the biggest brands in the industry, meaning you could be jetting off to your dream destination before you know it!" Head to www.anyworkanywhere.com for more.

- **Student Work Abroad Program (SWAP).** Note: this is limited to Canadian nationals only. "SWAP Working Holidays is a not-for-profit organization that has been working for over 40 years to promote cultural exchange opportunities to Canadians….Since SWAP's beginning, we have always been fully owned by Canadian students. We are a program of the Canadian Federation of Students, a not-for-profit organization that devotes their time and energy to student issues and concerns." See swap.ca for more.
- **Sadhana Village (India).** With this volunteer opportunity located outside of Mumbai, you can help with, "Adults with special needs and long and short-term service volunteers live and work together as equals in extended family homes throughout Sadhana Village." Visit http://sadhana-village.org/ for more details on ways you can help.
- **Agatha Amani House (Kenya).** "Volunteers and Interns will learn and gain a huge amount from volunteering at AAH and while doing so, will help support both the charity and the women and their babies and children. Volunteers are also welcome to contribute Ideas on how to get social enterprise programs started. Programs that are in the process of starting are, baking, crocheting and soap making. You will also be able to help with art, yoga, music and health and personal development classes plus social work." Visit www.agathaamanihouse.org

- **Ban Nai Soi Community Learning Center (Thailand).** "The primary goal of the Ban Nai Soi Community Learning Center (BNSCLC) is to provide a high school level education and key language skills to students currently living in the Mae Hong Son area. The school's curriculum focuses on English, Burmese, and Thai languages, organic farming, computer skills, Community Development and management . It is our hope that this education will give the students the opportunity to become valuable and successful leaders and educators within their communities."

Au Pair

Au Pairing, or nannying, is one of the most popular ways to see the world for free. You can volunteer your time to help care for kids in family homes across the world. Many families are overburdened with work and could use a responsible helper to pick up their kids, help with meals and even teach them another language. Keep in mind this option is almost exclusively limited to females.

- **AuPair.com.** "AuPair.com is one of the world's biggest Au Pair matching platforms, giving the opportunity to everyone to enter the amazing world of Au Pairing! Beyond the chance to find out if your potential Au Pair or Host Family is interested in you, with a Basic profile AuPair.com offers you useful articles and blog posts for both Au Pairs and Host Families, which will help you getting to know more about the program." Find your dream family abroad with AuPair.com now!
- **GreatAuPair.com.** "Since 2001, we've helped over 1,000,000 families and care providers safely connect online for local and international jobs. GreatAuPair.com is the original and most trusted international job matching service used by families to find affordable, trustworthy caregivers, providing a safe place to easily connect, get advice and hire with confidence. The

company provides a valuable service through the entire life cycle of a family from childcare, special needs care, pet sitting, tutoring, personal assistants, housekeeping to senior care." See https://www.greataupair.com/ to start now.

Birthright Programs

While this isn't technically a volunteer opportunity, getting in touch with your roots is a great way to reach fulfilment - and you can always find local volunteer programs once you arrive! Here are some opportunities to travel back to your homeland.

- **Reconnect Hungary.** "Reconnect Hungary, a program of the hungarian human rights foundation, is a unique cultural, educational and social immersion program for young adults aged 18-28 of Hungarian heritage, born in the U.S. or Canada." If you're Hungarian and under 28 years old, visit https://reconnecthungary.org/ to explore further.
- **National Hellenic Society.** "The Heritage Greece Program (HG) is a two-week cultural and educational immersion odyssey for accomplished Greek American college students who share their experience with a peer group of exceptional students from the American College of Greece (ACG) in Athens, Greece. The HG Program's goal is to reconnect the participants with their heritage, roots, language, history, and traditions. They have a once in a lifetime opportunity to explore their culture, as well as to identity and learn about the ancient past within the prism and context of modern Greece." See www.nationalhellenicsociety.org/ for more details.
- **Birthright Armenia.** "Birthright Armenia was founded in 2003 by Edele Hovnanian with the belief that it is every Armenian's birthright to not only see Armenia, but also experience their homeland via an enriching, hands-on, life-changing experience. Right from the start we believed that an immersion program in

Armenia with volunteer service at its core, especially one that encourages longer-term stays, would foster a greater sense of commitment to things Armenians and result in inspired and well-prepared young people to lead the next generation." Visit www.birthrightarmenia.org/en/ for more.

- **Birthright Israel.** "Birthright Israel aims to ensure a vibrant future of the Jewish people by strengthening Jewish identity, Jewish communities and connections with Israel via a trip to Israel for the majority of Jewish young adults from around the world. Our hope is that our trips motivate young people to continue to explore their Jewish identity and support for Israel and maintain long-lasting connections with the Israelis they meet on their trip. We encourage our alumni to take active roles in Jewish organizations and to participate in follow-up activities worldwide." If you're Jewish and want to connect to your roots, see https://www.birthrightisrael.com/ to get started.

Medical

Doctors and nurses are in great need around the world. So many face health complications in third world countries due to food shortages, famines, starvation, inadequate nutrient intake, injury and more. If you want to help make a difference abroad - or even in the U.S. - and you have medical qualifications, the following programs are for you.

- **Travel Nursing.** "Travel nursing allows you to explore the country whether you prefer beaches to mountains or cities to small towns. We have travel assignments in all 50 states — the hardest part is deciding where to go next." See www.travelnursing.org for more details.
- **Operation Smile.** "Operation Smile medical programs are almost entirely volunteer-based, so we rely on medical professionals who can take charge of their roles with confidence, conviction and world-class skill. These traits have

made Operation Smile a global leader in performing safe cleft surgery in resource-limited environments for more than three decades. Guided by our Global Standards of Care, medical volunteers must be able to work as a team to balance the highest possible quality of care with the efficiency to serve as many patients as our time and resources will allow. This demands stamina – physically, mentally and emotionally – as long hours and a fast pace are expected of our volunteers. Our work also requires travel to locations across the globe, which presents its own set of demands and challenges." If you've got the qualifications, apply at www.operationsmile.org

House Sitting

- **HouseCarers.com.** "Join fellow Global Citizens, Fulfilling their travel Dreams, OR free yourself from the burden and responsibilities of home, and pet ownership for a while for your well-earned trip away. This unbelievable opportunity, unheard by many, seems "too good to be true" - but it is!" Start house sitting at https://www.housecarers.com/
- **TrustedHouseSitters.com.** This isn't so much house sitting; it's more caring for people's pets while they're away. But, you can earn a place to stay in the process. "Every day, we connect thousands of home and pet owners with care-orientated sitters who will look after their home and pets for free, in exchange for a place to stay." Create your profile now ar https://www.trustedhousesitters.com/

Teaching English

English language teachers are in high demand around the world - afterall, it is the world's *lingua franca.* Because of this, you'll find there are plenty of opportunities for you to travel for free as an English teacher. Many opportunities are for payment (which I've covered in-depth in my other book on jobs that pay you to travel), but in this section all these opportunities are on a volunteer-only basis (this usually means you must be a fluent or native speaker and don't necessarily have to have formal teaching qualifications. This is a great way to see if teaching is right for you!):

- **Diverbo.** Want a free week of travel (or more)? Use your English language skills to help others learn and travel for free! "Volunteers can enjoy a free week at one of our English-speaking villages. Our venues host English "talkathons" every week and we sponsor native English-speakers to be the protagonists! A fun and rewarding experience is offered in exchange for your English conversation." See www.diverbo.com for more.
- **Sudan Volunteer Programme.** "Sudan Volunteer Programme (SVP) is a London and Khartoum-based charitable organisation sending graduates and near-graduates to Sudan to teach English at public higher education institutions around the country." www.svp-uk.com
- **Olancho Aid Foundation (Honduras).** "Two distinct volunteer programs help the Foundation accomplish its goals: the traditional volunteer program and the strategic advisor volunteer program. The traditional program focuses on community, spirituality, social justice, and simple living. It is a cultural exchange program that allows students to practice English with native-English speakers and offers volunteers opportunities for personal, professional, and spiritual growth. The strategic advisor program is geared toward experienced professionals and experts in their field who work to fill a specific, immediate need in the Foundation. Advisors serve as leaders and mentors within the Foundation administration." Learn more at https://olanchoaid.org.

- **Peace and Happiness Foundation (Thailand).** "These are the basic skills that are very important to help Thailand advance into the stage where all the developed countries stand. Peace And Happiness Foundation, therefore, was established in order to provide free education to the poor and underprivileged children so that they have a chance to develop analytical thinking skills and English abilities by bringing international learning system into the Thai schools for the poor..." Learn more at http://peaceandhappiness.org/
- **Vietnam Volunteering Organization.** "We strive to make English language education and exchange cultures available to everyone regardless of their economic status or background. We provide free, low cost and subsidized classes to our community and to anyone looking to improve their English skills, get a better job and have a brighter future." While this is listed under Teaching English, there are plenty of other opportunities. You can also help with marketing, social media, film making, graphic design and events. If you want to brush up on your skills for a good cause, visit vietnamvolunteering.org
- **TAPIF (France).** "The Teaching Assistant Program in France offers you the opportunity to work in France for 7 months, teaching English to French students of all ages. Each year, over 1,500 American citizens and permanent residents teach in public schools across all regions of metropolitan France and in the overseas departments of France such as French Guiana, Guadeloupe, Martinique and Réunion. The American cohort is part of the larger Assistants de langue en France program, which recruits 4,500 young educators from 60 countries to teach 15 languages annually in France." Visit tapif.org to apply now!

Tour Group and Cruise Leader

Volunteering isn't always about teaching English to impoverished kids or restoring the environment. Sometimes it can be about teaching others about a different culture or history. If you want to travel for free, you can do so by leading tour groups and even working on cruise ships.

- **All Aboard Travel.** "You may have overheard a friend or colleague bragging that they went on a great cruise vacation for FREE. Now you can too! If you are the "group leader" who organizes friends ,or family or a group to sail on the same cruise departure you can be rewarded with discounted pricing, special amenities and even a complimentary cruise fare." allaboardtravel.com.
- **Hf Holidays.** "Do you love to get your boots on, grab a map and head out into the great outdoors? How about staying in fantastic walking locations, with great local food and a wonderful sociable atmosphere? Would you like to lead groups of like-minded people and share your knowledge of the countryside in destinations across the UK and beyond? If this sounds like your idea of a good time, then we may have just the opportunity for you! We are looking for volunteers to lead walking holidays at our 18 UK country houses and across Europe. You'd be joining a team of over 800 enthusiastic, experienced and sociable walkers who help share great experiences with over 60,000 guests each year." www.hfholidays.co.uk.
- **Select International Tours.** Select operates religious tours for those who would like to do a pilgrimage. "Do you have a group of 10 or more family and friends who want to go on pilgrimage? Then you have a group! learn the benefits of leading a group with select." Visit partners.selectinternationaltours.com/ for more.

- **Grand Circle Cruise Line and Travel.** "Bring at least 10 friends or family with you on any Grand Circle Land Tour or River Cruise and you'll travel FREE as the Group Leader. Or, you may choose to share the cash equivalent of your FREE trip amongst the members of your group—that way, everyone saves." See www.gct.com for more details.
- **Merit Group Travel.** "If you are a group leader, free travel is possible depending on your group's size. Typically we build in free travel for the group leader for groups over ten but in reality the number of free group leaders can be customized to suit your needs." www.meritgrouptravel.com
- **Cha Educational Tours.** "Earn a free trip for yourself by enrolling just six students on a CHA tour! Earn additional free trips by increasing your group size, or collect an unlimited stipend for every traveler not credited towards a free trip. (As a special welcome to CHA, those first-time group leaders unable to recruit six students will travel free with just five!) And, if you recruit fewer than six travelers, you will still enjoy a generous discount off of the regular tour price." www.cha-tours.com/
- **EF Educational Tours.** "You've taught your students about the world—now make the world their classroom. With EF, you can give your students the opportunity of travel, and always at the lowest price. Enroll just six students and your spot is covered. Plus, for every six additional travelers you can bring a chaperone for free." See their website for more details at: www.eftours.com/
- **Explorica.** "New to Explorica? Qualify to attend our Program Leader Training and get to know the company on a free trip. Meet other teachers who love to travel, get insider tips from Explorica staff and a veteran Program Leader on leading student tours, and still have plenty of time to explore on your own." Visit www.explorica.com for more.

Wildlife and Environmental Conservation

Since we only have one Earth, we can help make the world we all live in a better place by volunteering to protect nature and all of its living creatures. Whether you want to work with turtles and endangered species, plant trees, or educate others about limiting plastics, there are plenty of different types of volunteer programs to be discovered.

- **Turtle Island Restoration Network.** "Turtle Island Restoration Network was launched by a dedicated and talented team of volunteers working together to save sea turtles. Today, we have multiple locations and many opportunities for you to get involved in ocean advocacy." For more information, visit seaturtles.org/take-action/volunteer/
- **Sea Turtle Conservancy.** "Go wild with sea turtles! Experience sustainable travel with a splash of conservation, go on a guided walk to watch a sea turtle laying eggs in the Archie Carr Refuge, or get the chance to see a sea turtle being released in the morning as part of the Tour de Turtles by taking part in a Sea Turtle Experience with the Sea Turtle Conservancy." More information is available at www.conserveturtles.org
- **Conservation Volunteers Australia.** "Conservation Volunteers welcomes everyone who shares our love of nature and commitment to conserving the environment. Not only that, there are many benefits to becoming an environmental volunteer such as learning new skills, improving health and well-being, and developing a sense of place in your local community – what's not to love!" https://conservationvolunteers.com.au/
- **Centro de Conservación de la Biodiversidad Chiloé-Silvestre (Chile).** Help educate others and preserve the natural biodiversity found in Chile with this amazing program. If you want to join, you'll be provided with accomodation with

other volunteers. You must stay for a minimum of 2 weeks. For more details, visit http://chiloesilvestre.cl/

In-Kind and Donations

In the previous section, we covered ways you can pair your travels with helping others in exchange for free room and board. Now, we'll look at the inverse of that experience: relying on the generosity of others so that you can travel the world for free. There are nice people in the world who want to help people travel since it's so transformative. In exchange, you may be expected to share your beliefs, opinions and outlook on the world with hosts on Couchsurfing, for example. Or, if you receive a donation from others, you may feel called upon to make your travel experience more meaningful by interacting with locals, stepping out of your comfort zone and learning a new language as you travel. But, make no mistake: just because generous people may help you with room and board and funds for your travels, that doesn't mean you should take advantage of their generosity and treat your trip as a vacation. If you want to grow spiritually and expand your perception of the world, you must travel and not vacation.

In this section, I'll go over two ways you can leverage help from others to travel for free (or nearly free):

1. **Couchsurfing.** Couchsurfing is the crazy (or not-so-crazy) idea of staying with complete strangers around the world who may or may not share your same beliefs, values and outlook on the world. I first tried Couchsurfing when I was 19 years old and have since had eight experiences with Couchsurfing.com. I'll outline the pros and cons of traveling with this method and let you in on some of my Couchsurfing stories.
2. **Donations.** It may seem wild, but there are people willing to give you money to travel. The first people you should contact are the ones in your close circle: friends and family. For example, when I went on a religious trip to Honduras, we were required to write "donation letters" to help raise funds. From there, you may consider setting up a profile on a website like Gofundme.com to help fund your travels. But be sure your intentions for traveling are clear - why should someone donate to your travels? How will you use your travel experience - for selfish reasons, or to benefit those around you?

Shake Up Your Understanding of the World

When you stay with someone else it'll be hard not to change. You'll disagree. You may end up talking casually about the weather and touristic sites. Or, you may end up discussing deep things like the meaning of life, politics, and morality. The bottom line is Couchsurfing will shake up your understanding of the world. You'll be confronted with completely different viewpoints and beliefs from your own which is a good thing. So often, we live in information bubbles and don't often hear opinions from the other side. We write off people who hold different beliefs from our own as "ignorant," "conspiracy theorists" or even downright dumb. But, is that really true? Can you find common ground with people who are seemingly very different from you? Ultimately, that's the beauty of Couchsurfing: you're forced to connect with people on a deeper level. Beyond the robotic "How are you?" "Good, thanks." Couchsurfing gives users the opportunity to break free from robotic conversations and interact with others different from ourselves.

Restore Your Faith in Humanity

Each and every time a host hands me their keys on Couchsurfing I'm blown away. It amazes me how much faith many Couchsurifng hosts have in Couchsurfers, and that, in turn, inspires me to have more faith in others. So much so that I often leave my laptop on the table when I get up to use the bathroom in a cafe and I now give people time when asking for directions on the street (whereas before I'd assume that almost everyone has bad intentions). That doesn't mean that I'm naive - bad people do exist. But, it means that if someone were to pick up my laptop and try to run off with it while I'm in the bathroom, I'm sure that someone would step up and say something - as I would for someone else in this situation (plus, my laptop is a Google Chromebook - I got it for just over $100, anyway!) We hear bad news on a daily basis - don't forget to count the acts of kindness you experience from strangers on a daily basis. From opening the door to you, to being patient with you as a tourist, to a random, warm smile from a stranger.

Couchsurfing

Skills Needed	No technical skills required, but you do need people skills. Primarily open-mindedness and flexibility - afterall, you'll be living with a complete stranger.
Hours Per Week	None. But, do expect to interact with your hosts. Some will offer you a tour and expect you to hangout with them, others will be extremely laid-back and let you come and go as you please.
Requirements and Restrictions	Required to set up an account on Couchsurfing.com. If no hosts contact you, you may be required to send out requests to hosts.
Location	Worldwide.

Before I actually used the Couchsurfing app for myself, I first learned about it when I was still in high school. It planted a seed in my mind that I first thought was strange, but that seed has blossomed into me becoming a frequent user of the platform. The thought of using Couchsurfing never crossed my mind until I met two extraordinarily brave Chinese women who visited as guest speakers during my time as an event coordinator on the Programming and Diversity Board while in community college. We received these two guest speakers during our training retreat. These two were traveling all throughout Latin America on bicycles; they even ended up all the way in my little town of Bellingham, Washington. What was even more crazy to me at the time: they stayed with people on Couchsurfing.com. How could they be so trusting of complete strangers?

At the time I thought that was slightly naive and maybe even dangerous. You never know who you are going to stay with and what can happen, right? I thought to myself: 'That sounds like a nice way to travel for free...but what if something bad happens?' But then a paradigm shift occurred: if you can survive living in a room full of bunks (sometimes up to 12 beds in one room, with one bathroom like I did in Miami…yikes!) with complete strangers in a hostel, then surely you can survive a stay with a host in their home. Or Airbnb. I've stayed in rooms rented out on Airbnb and have come out in one piece. Bad things can happen - as they can when you walk down the street or drive a car - but they rarely do. Now that I've used the platform several times, I think Couchsurfing.com is a great place to meet travelers who are like-minded and understand wanderlust and the journey. These are people who want to support you as you explore what the world has to offer. Many of those who start out surfing turn to hosting (like myself; I plan on hosting travellers in the future once I've settled in one place for a while). Couchsurfing is great, and the set-up is super easy; there is even a mobile app so you can use it on the go. While I may have made it sound like you find a host everywhere you go, this isn't always the case (especially when travelling outside of the big city). I'll explain how to increase the odds a host accepts your reservation request and let you in on some of my (crazy) stories I had while using Couchsurfing so you know if it's right for you.

Getting Started On Couchsurfing

In theory, all you have to do is put in a quick little blurb and upload some photos (I suggest uploading 3 or more so that hosts can "read" you better. Add a selfie, some pictures from your travels and maybe even a picture with friends to express your social and fun). But in practice, there's a lot more to it than just filling out some forms and uploading photos - you're essentially creating a "portfolio" of yourself and as you create your portfolio, you must approach it from the host's perspective: hosts want trustworthy, interesting and respectful guests. Is that the message your profile conveys? You have to realize: hosts are inundated with couchsurfing requests almost every day. You need to ensure you stand out. Treat your profile as if it were an application to one of the volunteer programs or a more casual job interview. Show your personality and your passion for travel and highlight some interesting things about yourself. But also, don't forget to express your gratitude and mention that you're a clean, tidy and respectful person (Which you should be if you're planning on staying at someone's place as a guest!)

I've gotten a place to stay in almost every city I've travelled to. Here's how you can boost your profile to increase your chances, too:

- **Use clear photos of your face.** Did you read that? Of your face! Not of your dog, the sunset or an interesting building. You need to include a face picture; we're human beings. We respond better and trust someone much more when we know what they look like. Surprisingly, many haven't understood this and continue to use impersonal photos.

- **Fill out all sections.** Your profile on Couchsurfing is broke down into the following sections: About me; Why I'm on Couchsurfing; Interests; Music, Movies and Books; One amazing thing I've done; Teach, Learn, Share; What I can share with hosts; Countries I've visited; Countries I've lived in. As you can see, there's lots of room to give detailed information about your life, your travels and your interests. Be specific and generous with what you share. That way, something you write is bound to connect with a potential host.
- **Express easy-goingness, trust and gratefulness.** So many Couchsurfers don't appreciate hosts. They write generic requests (something I've never done) that they copy and paste to hosts without reading their profiles. Don't do that on yours. You want to show that you're grateful for the experience to Couchsurf (afterall, it'll save you hundreds or even thousands of dollars on accomodation) and also that you're a 'go with the flow' type of person.
- **Don't be generic.** What do hosts get out of hosting? They get to experience and interact with someone who's different than them. So don't be afraid to express yourself and pour yourself into your profile. Put some effort into it. Couchsurfing isn't Airbnb or a hotel; it's an experience. You want to make sure it's clear that you're willing to converse and share with hosts as a cultural exchange and aren't just using them for a free place to stay.

As I said, most hosts are the types that want to help out the travel community, so put a little effort into your description and interactions with hosts. Your reward will be 10 fold! Not only will you have free accommodation and a tour guide, you can also potentially gain a life long friend. To rephrase: don't treat Couchsurfing as solely a place to crash for free; it's much more about the experience and connecting with somebody different around the world.

How I Started Using Couchsurfing

During my two-week spring break vacation while I was studying in Belgium, I bought some dirt cheap tickets to Romania, Rome and Ibiza and Barcelona, Spain. I simply created a "Public Trip" by entering in the dates of my travels as well as a description of what I was planning on seeing there and how I'd provide a fun, valuable experience for hosts (i.e. I proposed that we could go for a walk and see the city, grab a drink and some local bites, etc.) and the offers came flooding in. Well, not exactly flooding in, but I did receive about 5 per destination (tons in Barcelona and upwards of 20 invitations in London! Moral of the story: you'll always get more offers in big cities than in smaller, less-traveled towns, unsurprisingly), and the ability to choose between hosts was great but almost overwhelming since there were so many.

I quickly realized that travel - even if staying in hostels - can add up quickly. In fact, I was actually set on using hostels for this trip I had planned for spring break, which were all under $15 per night...except in one city: Rome! I looked up hostel beds for Rome and almost everything was booked. I think there were just about two or three options that were around $40 which was far over my budget and, in fact, cost more than my ticket! But, I had already (foolishly) booked the ticket and was determined to go still. Sleeping on the street wasn't an option, and neither was a paid accommodation since I was already at the top of my budget. Alas, I turned to the internet and reflected on the two Chinese girls who came to visit. That seed that was planted grew roots in mind. I decided I'd finally be crazy enough to use Couchsurfing. And so I did. While my original decision to use couchsurfing was based on finances, over the years that I've used Couchsurfing, I've learned to appreciate it for what it is and almost all of my experiences have been positive. Yes - you save money on accommodation and it's nice to travel free. But, that's not the point. You also gain an experience that's far more authentic when you stay with someone else. The hosts I've stayed with on Couchsurfing have been extremely helpful and welcoming. Sure, I've had one bad experience and there are some creepy profiles on Couchsurfing (which I'll cover later), but for the most part, it's been a fun experience to take part in and I'm glad I started becoming an active user.

Some Couchsurfing Stories: From Rome, to London to Brussels

After spending an amazing time exploring the old city in Bucharest, Romania, it was time to move on to my next destination: Rome. I was a little bit nervous since I'd be using Couchsurfing for the first time, but my host and I stayed in contact via WhatsApp for a few days before I flew there so I felt more at ease (though that didn't stop me from booking a hostel room for one night, even though it was $40. Just in case!) Fortunately, my couchsurfing experience went extremely well in Rome as a then Couchsurfing virgin. As soon as I landed in Rome, I used the wifi from the station to let the host know that I was coming and all went well. Everything was set. It was a little inconvenient because he wasn't available until after 6 pm (which is one thing to keep in mind: unlike a hotel or an Airbnb, your schedule revolves around your host's schedule. That's why flexibility is so important!) so I walked around and explored the city on my own, carrying my backpack along (that's why it's important to pack light!) until he was free. But honestly, this was no biggie. Just a minor inconvenience and something to keep in mind when using Couchsurfing: you're the guest, so you play by the host's rules and schedule.

We met in one of the fancy, touristy areas of Rome where he was finishing up some work since he rents out apartments on Airbnb. He gave me a tour of one of the places he rents out and then from there we cruised off straight away to explore the enchanting streets of Rome!

That's one of the biggest advantages of using Couchsurfing. Your host is a local. He or she knows all the ins and outs of the city so you get a much more unique, authentic experience. Couchsurfing is a great way to connect with people who are usually willing to show you the true culture of the destination you're visiting and let you in on all the hottest spots that you may miss if you are traveling solo.

We cruised those streets in his little Fiat (which almost gave me a heart attack - the drivers in Rome are crazy!) and bounced from the Trevi Fountain to the Pantheon to the Colosseum and finished up with an aperitivo (which is an alcoholic drink you drink right before dinner paired with buffet style snacks. The best thing in the world! There's also something called "Apericena" which is an aperitivo but with a more filling buffet that you eat for dinner. If you're visiting Italy, indulging in an aperitivo or apericena is a must!). After exploring and filling our bellies, we went back to the house where I stayed on his very comfortable couch (and passed out after the exhausting flight and delicious food). Honestly, the couch was a lot more comfortable than the majority of the hostel beds I have stayed in!

The next day, my host went to work and left me in the apartment. I decided to go off and explore Rome on my own for the rest of the day. From what I recall, I didn't get an apartment key (which is fine. Most of the time, however, hosts do give you an extra set of keys) which is one of the drawbacks sometimes. That means if you want to come back and rest in the apartment if you're jet lagged or tired from all the walking, you can't. You'll need to find a park or a cafe to relax and sit down for a while. If you're in an arrangement like this where you're not given a key, once you're out, you're out. Be sure you take everything with you (water bottle, phone charger, umbrella, jacket for night, etc.) and have anything you need as you probably won't be getting back in until later. The host and I got along fine. He even provided food for a few meals which I was extremely grateful for. As I mentioned before, it's extremely important to practice gratitude and be flexible. This person is entrusting you and inviting you into their home and often wants to teach you about their cultures and learn about yours. Respect that and practice all those manners your mama taught you! Be clean, be respectful, offer to help around the houses and do the dishes, cook your own food without making a mess. And you should always buy your own food without expecting your Couchsurfing host to cook for you (which I've read is common among some Couchsurfers, unfortunately. Never expect a free meal! It's common, but don't insist). However, many hosts will cook for you or invite you to a meal at a local restaurant which is never a bad thing since you're getting free (and usually delicious) food!

Some Not So Pleasant Couchsurfing Experiences...

Please be careful of the weirdos, freaks and flakes that are on Couchsurfing, just like they exist in the real world. Thankfully Couchsurfing has a review system in place where past surfers and hosts can leave reviews, in addition to the photos so you can get a 'feel' for who your host is and whether they'll be creepy or normal, interesting people. Following my excellent experience on Couchsurfing in Rome, I was ready to delete my account and never use it again (in fact, I didn't use it until I needed to save money on accommodation in expensive London. Unfortunately, I had a terrible experience). Following my trip in Rome, my last two interactions with Couchsurfing weren't exactly pleasant. After flying back to the US during my studies in Belgium, I tried Couchsurfing in Miami during high season in April i.e. when prices are at their peak and hostels are normally full in South Beach. I did get some offers, especially around Mid Beach and Bal Harbor areas which are north of Miami Beach, but those options were far from where I wanted to stay (again, another thing to keep in mind: you don't have a say in where your hosts live. If you want to stay comfortably in the center of the city, you'll either need to be lucky and find a host that lives there or get a hotel!) Sometimes the only viable options may be out of the city center, far from where you'd like to be which is why you should always have a backup plan and never expect too much from hosts out of Couchsurfing. If it takes you over an hour to get to the center of the city, it may not be worth it to use Couchsurfing for your trip.

I did get some offers from hosts in South Beach, but unfortunately most of the offers were from creepy dudes that explicitly stated they are "nudists" and nudity is required. One profile even announced that you are required to sleep in the bed with them and that they 'wank' every night, which is just as hilarious as it is creepy. Personally, I have nothing against people that choose to partake in it and I would feel comfortable with someone who genuinely lives a nudist lifestyle, but sleeping next to someone who claims they wank on their profile is not exactly pleasant (thanks, but no thanks!). So this is, of course, something to keep in mind. Fortunately these types of people are few and far between and you'll most likely have a creep-free experience (except in Miami Beach, apparently!) Needless to say, I declined all offers from hosts in Miami Beach and fortunately s friend of mine let me crash at their place for a couple nights before I flew back to my hometown.

That's one of the unfortunate drawbacks of Couchsurfing, and life in general: some people will always try to take advantage of you and your situation. You're young and want to travel the world; many will want to help you along your journey with honest intentions and a desire to connect with people from different cultures, while others will try to take advantage of the situation. Profiles that use nudity or refer to sexual things are a no-go in my book. It's not worth it to be exploited due to being young and broke. Many older men use Couchsurfing to take advantage of young travelers (both young women and men if they are gay). Always check the reviews to ensure you're not put in an awkward position.

Creepers are something to keep on your radar when using Couchsurfing, but you also have to be on the lookout with people who are simply incompatible with you or expect too much from you. What do I mean by this? I'll tell you about my experience in London to explain (by the way, I don't want to make it sound like Couchsurinfg is all bad. It's not. This was the only person I stayed with out of seven who made me feel uncomfortable). Prior to heading to London from Rome where I was studying at the time, everything seemed fine from the host. In fact, he had over 300 reviews with only about 10 being negative. In retrospect, I should have probably read between the lines. Even the positive reviews hinted that the guy was very strict and slightly creepy. The host was located in the center of London in an enormous, beautiful flat. As soon as I got there, I could tell he was a bit of a control freak and kept commenting on my appearance in a way that was starting to get uncomfortable. But I simply smiled and said 'thanks' and changed the subject. It wasn't anything too bad and more comments were made during the entirety of my stay. Things did start to get weird when the guy referred to me leaving my zipped backpack on the bed as looking like a 'refugee camp'. I had literally set my backpack down after arriving and thought nothing of it. Apparently leaving the backpack on the bed instead of inside the closet looked like a 'refugee camp' to this very controlling, odd man. Later, he became literally irate when I left the closet door cracked instead of closed fully and in the following days he would relentlessly text me throughout the day (we're talking 3-10 messages per hour, every hour) followed by chains of question marks. Since I was out exploring the city I couldn't reply instantaneously due to not having wifi which he didn't seem to get. Oh, and I had to leave precisely at 9 am which wasn't stated before I got there. Since he was Italian and Italians are known to be flexible with their time, one morning I left at 9:01 am; as you can probably guess, things didn't go well. I received comments that I was 'making him late' and 'ruining his day' for simply leaving a minute late. Needless to say, it was a stressful experience and I felt constantly on edge. I didn't know what would set this irate man off who seemed to be looking for any excuse to criticize and lose his temper. After just a few days I decided I couldn't take it anymore and stayed elsewhere. The thing with Couchsurfing is that many young travelers are exploited in a way and pressured into leaving positive reviews so that they are viewed as being 'grateful', which they should be. But it's important to be honest as well. This was the first time I left a bad review since I'm not one to bite my tongue. The fancy and extremely luxurious centrally-located flat probably created a 'halo-effect' for many travelers, but not for me. I wanted to warn others of what they could expect when they stayed at this host's place. For me, I'd rather spend money in a hostel than stay in a luxury flat with miserable company.

To emphasize again: this was my only poor experience I had staying with someone on Couchsurfing. Would I use Couchsurfing again? Yes, in a heartbeat (though I took a break from it for a long time after London and was determined not to use it again). There are definitely some creepers out there who want to take advantage of attractive, young travellers in exchange for accommodation. But then, there are those who host travelers out of kindness and compassion - and they are the majority. My last stay in London was just a bad, OCD, controlling draw from the bag. If anything, the poor experience taught me to be a bit more cautious and inquire about any rules before staying with someone so I get a feel for who the person is. Be selective and cautious of who you are staying with. Check out their pictures, read their reviews and see what guests who have stayed with them have reviewed. Be sure that you read their profile carefully. Don't just glance at it and skim the details and reviews. Read it.

Making Lifelong Friends and Memories

After the bad experience in London, I rejected the idea of using Couchsurfing. But then my grandma wanted to come visit me in Italy and my mind changed. After nearly a year passed, I figured I'd check couchsurfing again to avoid paying for an expensive hostel or Airbnb in

Brussels where I needed to meet my grandma. I rewrote my profile with more details about myself and what I expected from Couchsurfing (making it clear that I'm open-minded and love to travel, but I'm not on Couchsurfing to be taken advantage of) and created a Public Trip in Brussels. A host reached out to me who was from Switzerland and worked in the government. He seemed very interesting - and he was - so I was excited to meet him even if it was just for one night (since I was meeting my grandma the next morning in the airport). We met after he got off work and explored the city, grabbed a beer and had awesome conversations. This experience made me fall in love with Couchsurfing again. I realized the good hosts far outweigh and outnumber the bad. While we had a short experience, we still stay in touch periodically to this day, and I stayed at his place again for just one night when I passed through Brussels for a flight in Paris (yes, my life is complicated and I'm always traveling!).

After that, I spent the summer in Italy and Croatia where I met some fantastic hosts. One host in Trieste took me to a pizzeria with his friends one night in the Slovenian-speaking part of Trieste in the hills. We met with his friends and it was an unforgettable night! After dinner, we also got to see thousands of bugs that glow in the dark (fireflies) which was the first time I had seen so many all in one place! This host also drove me around in his car to the church that overlooked the city, providing spectacular views of the glowing tiled rooftops and peaceful waves of the Adriatic sea. I felt so grateful; these are the types of experiences you'd never be a part of unless you meet a local. So clearly, Couchsurfing isn't all bad. You'll make plenty of memories and see parts of destinations you'd never know exist. Later, I used Couchsurfing again and stayed with a professor and his daughter in Padova for a few days where I got a real, authentic look into the region of Veneto. Instead of going to Venice, we headed to a lesser-known fishing village south of the tourist-ridden destination: Chioggia. There were virtually no tourists when we got there, and the small town also has canals and bridges just like Venice (though not as many, of course). We also grabbed some local bites and bought some fish for the dinner we cooked together later on.

Beyond that summer in Italy, I also used Couchsurfing for the entirety of my travels in the south of Spain (Andalucia) and in Las Palmas. I stayed with one host in February who had a fantastic rooftop apartment where I soaked up the warm Andalusian sun after spending a cold winter completing my internship in Turin. The host was very nice, too! We had frequent coffees together and chatted lots. He even provided me with food for breakfast and we cooked most of our dinners together (which I was very grateful for). I was given a key and was free to come and go as I pleased, so I would head out to the city to find relaxing cafes to work in and walk along the beach. After I got tired, I'd head back to the rooftop apartment and fall asleep in the lounge chair on the terrace. While that trip may not have been as adventurous as my trip in Italy, it was relaxing and I had great conversations with the Couchsurfing hosts.

To sum up, most of the hosts are extremely pleasant and very generous. You'll surely make life-long memories and travel more authentically than if you were to travel alone and stay in hostels. If you're hesitant to use Coushduring - don't be! Just exercise caution, read profiles carefully and don't stay withrude, expecting hosts - even if they live in Central London!

Get Started on Couchsurfing Now

1. Create your profile. As mentioned, creating your profile is pretty quick and easy. Just be sure you fill out all of the categories completely so that hosts know who they're dealing with. Be yourself, but convey that you're trustworthy and easy to get along with.
2. Plan your trip in advance. Be sure you don't become a habitual last-minute couchsurfer. Try to find a host and book your

Couchsurfing experience at least a week or two before you plan on traveling. Sometimes what I do is add the hosts as friends even months before visiting a destination to keep them on your radar and express your interest.

3. Write tailored stay requests. Since Couchsurfing is about a shared experience rather than an impersonal Airbnb or hotel experience, you must write a tailored request. If you see something on their profile that catches your eye, let them know. Writing about shared interests is a great way to break the ice - and will surely increase your chances of being accepted.
4. Be a good guest. Not only should you be a good, respectful and clean person in general, but also because your review depends on it. This is especially important if you don't have many reviews; even one bad review can permanently sour your Couchsurfing reputation.

Crowdfunding

Skills Needed	Writing and marketing skills to get your campaign out there and gain support.
Hours Per Week	You'll have to spend some initial time creating the campaign. After that, no time is required.
Requirements and Restrictions	A strong social network i.e. plenty of connections. It's also helpful if you have a moving story or purpose that inspires others.
Location	Anywhere.

Travel is the best education, as they say. And after studying in four different colleges and getting a Bachelor's degree in Business and Management, I can attest to this. I've learned far more from my travels than I ever did enclosed in the walls of my university. I consider travel a form of investment. Travel sparks self-improvement and self-awareness. It creates people who are better able to solve problems, who are more open minded to other cultures and differing mindsets and are better able to communicate. Travel allows new perspectives and gets you out of your comfort zone. Because travel is so transformative, family and friends would love to pour into helping you out. Usually, you need to have a reason to travel - like a mission trip or a volunteer trip, but many are open to the idea of helping you out just to see the world for no reason other than travel itself. A trip for the sole purpose of travel is just as worthy of donation as a volunteer trip, service trip, or college fund since travel creates better people; people who have the power to change the world around them.

If you want to leverage your network and see if your friends and family would be willing to help you out before you embark on your journey, simply sign up on Gofundme.com and create a profile and state your case. Why is it that you want to travel? How will it benefit you? How will you help others? How will you use what you learned to help the community and the world? Be as specific as possible. Don't be superficial. Go into depth about how you think travel will change you as a person and where you're planning on traveling. Travel isn't just about going to exotic places to get a tan, drink beer, and lounge around all day about the ocean. It's about finding yourself, connecting with others and overall growing as a person. Travel is one of the most fulfilling experiences available to us. If friends and family - and even complete strangers - do donate, treat it as a scholarship. It's not just free money; it's an opportunity to grow as a person. People love to help out and are willing to chip in a bit if you are travelling for self growth, in order to benefit others, or to cross something off your bucket list. Make a compelling backstory and broadcast it on social media and other outlets. While I have never used this method, you may have some success, and many other Gofundme users have used this quite effectively.

Just remember not to say you want to "vacation". You are not going to a resort and having access to everything as you would back home. Ensure that it is something that will grow you as a person and inspire others.

Some example titles of campaigns you could run are:

- "Fulfill my dream of summiting Mount Everest"
- "Need airplane ticket to Europe to study medicine and save lives"
- "Bucket list trip through South East Asia to help my depression"

See the difference? It's not just about funding a vacation (e.g. "Help Me Shop the Streets of Milano"), but rather about accomplishing a goal that leads to self-fulfillment and personal growth. GoFundMe is a great start since it's easy to use, but there are some drawbacks (namely its fees). The platform is smooth and easy to use, being connected directly with Facebook and Twitter. It is the #1 Crowdsourcing site on the internet. But, what many don't know is that GoFundMe makes some major profit off of its users, and takes a fairly steep cut of the donations you and others receive. To break down the pricing and fees, here is their current pricing for the United States as of May 1, 2020:

- 0% GoFundMe Platform (before it was 5%)
- 2.9% Transaction Fees
- $0.30 Per-Donation Fee

Those are pretty steep cuts into your donations! However, the advantage of using Gofundme is that it's well known and is incredibly user-friendly. It wouldn't be as easy creating your own website or your own social media page for your campaign (though it'd be worth it if you want to save 2.9% of the donations...plus 30 cents deducted each donation!) The main benefit is the name recognition and ease of use, as well as it being the #1 crowdfunding source. If you're looking for alternative, you may want to try:

- **FundMyTravel.com.** Unlike GoFundMe, FundMyTravel is just for travelers so you're not thrown in the mix with people raising money for medical bills, charities and other important needs. This way, when people visit FundMyTravels.com they know what they're getting themselves into: helping fund travelers' dreams to make a difference around the world. Setting up an account on FundMyTravel.com is easy - just keep in mind FundMyTravel takes 5% of all donations.
- **PayPal.** PayPal is free for those who have PayPal accounts. There may be a fee tacked on if one of the users who doesn't have a PayPal account sends funds to your PayPal account directly from their bank account. But, it's easily remediable: all they have to do is sign up for a Paypal account to avoid those fees.
- **Use your bank directly.** Ask for donations directly through your bank account using your account number. Be sure to include your story and make it seem as believable as possible. The benefit to using a platform is that it is much more 'put together' and makes donors feel their money is going to a legitimate cause.

How to Start a Successful Campaign Now

1. Figure out your story and why others should support you. Remember to express how meaningful travel would be for you and the ways you plan on using your experience to help others.
2. Determine whether you want to use Gofundme.com or go independently. Since Gofundme takes a cut of your donations, you may decide not to use the platform. Instead, you can create

your own webpage if you have basic web design knowledge on a platform like WordPress and use payment platforms like PayPal.me or your bank account directly.

3. Treat the funds as you would a scholarship. After getting some donations for your flight and accommodation, don't spend it all in one place as your mother should have told you! Try to make it last as long as possible, be reasonable and don't book any luxury hotels since it's less likely you'll grow and interact with locals on a vacation.

Costly Travel Programs to Avoid

The above methods of traveling the world for free are incredibly useful and often lead to personal growth and a changed perception of the world. Each one of them is legitimate and has been tried and tested. While many bloggers and authors often write about things that they have not experienced themselves, my goal was to provide anecdotal evidence and be as specific as possible so that you feel comfortable making the leap and getting out there in the world! But before ending the book, I wanted to take time to discuss something almost as important as the free travel opportunities themselves: opportunities to avoid. There are many bloggers, travel agencies and websites that exist to solely make money off of young people who want to travel the world. Many blog posts and websites include the information above, but they also include the following methods of "travel" which I wouldn't recommend at all.

You'll notice that I have no affiliate links above in the book and that I am not trying to push the idea of going on a for-profit excursion. In fact, all of the resources above are either sponsored by the government, organizations that are free to use or require a small fee (ee.g. Couchsurfing, WWOOFING, etc.) The methods that I'm going to mention are usually incredibly expensive and also very restrictive

(which means no room to go out and explore independently, defeating the whole purpose of travel!)

I'd Skip These Travel Opportunities

When young people type in "volunteer abroad" or "travel abroad" or something similar, they're almost always bound to come across these two types of trips. I did myself when I used to research ways to travel for free or cheap. Thankfully, I was smart enough to avoid the methods except for a mission trip I took when I was involved with a church (which had some benefits to it, but it was very pricy and I didn't feel it was moral to be staying in a luxury resort, being able to order anything off the menu while we were running a religious camp for impoverished kids. On top of that, I didn't have any flexibility over my schedule and felt a bit suffocated by the group I was with).

Religious Mission Trips

Religion is something that can be great and encourage growth from within, but as far as travelling goes, it's best not to mix travel and religion (at least in my opinion). Travel is about opening your mind to other ways of life; about walking in the shoes of others. Religion, on the other hand, restricts you from engaging in those experiences. For example, when I took a religious mission trip to Los Angeles where we helped serve meals in Skid Row and repair a church, we passed by a Church of Scientology in Hollywood and our group decided to go in. Many people said they felt "off" there, which is completely fine, but for curious individuals like me I approach people with different beliefs from a place of curiosity; not of criticism. While I have no interest in Scientology, I found it interesting that we couldn't explore further while we were there. Additionally, during another mission trip I went on to Honduras, we stayed in our group the entire time. Virtually no one branched out to interact with locals, other than the brief (and superficial, I felt) interactions we had with the kids at our camp and an orphanage. How can you grow when you're staying within your group and not interacting with others who are different from you? While some may not agree, it is my opinion that mission trips don't really allow you to fully partake in a culture. I'm saying this as somebody who has been on two mission trips in his life so far and has, for the most part, regretted them.

Another thing that I'm not a fan of when it comes to traveling with a mission trip group is that they tend to be very wasteful and expensive. I raised over $2000 in order to fly to Roatan, Honduras to serve the population there. But, I got a sour stomach during our 10 days there that lasted long after the experience. We went to a village about 10 minutes away by our private bus shuttle after eating breakfast served by the resort we were staying at (in addition, all of our meals were covered and we could eat anything off the restaurant menu at the beachfront resort) and hand out crackers and cheap juice to the kids there. I remember one of the "leaders" even complained that I gave the kids too many crackers. In my opinion, the roles should have been reversed: Give us the cheap juice and crackers and let our bellies grumble for a change. And the greatest irony of all is that Bellingham, Washington lies in a zone within the US dubbed the "Land of the Nones" meaning people increasingly don't identify with any religion at all; a stark contrast to Honduras's zealous Catcholic community. It seems the religious group should have learned more about Christianity from the locals rather than trying to preach it, given that the community seems to be more numerous there while people in the Pacific Northwest tend to be non-religious. With that $2000, I could have booked a *real* service trip for months - including airfare! But the trip emphasized modern comforts and vacation rather than real acts of service. All in all, I wasn't impressed by the wasteful spending. Sure, I got to see the world and learned tremendously from both experiences (in fact, my trip to Honduras was the reason I got my passport. For that, I'm grateful!), but

I can't help but to think I would have gotten more from the experiences and been more impactful had I ventured out alone.

The trip to Disneyland we took was loads of fun in LA, but what does that have to do with helping alleviate poverty and providing meals? The fancy meals and snorkeling excursions were spectacular in Roatan, Honduras, but what about the starving kids and infested, unneutered dogs? Why was the money we raised not used towards the population we intended to serve? Those are the questions I'm stuck wondering to myself and are the reasons I don't recommend traveling with any religious group. If you want to volunteer somewhere abroad, stick to the Peace Corps or organize a help exchange experience. Your money will go a longer way and you'll make a far greater impact.

For-Profit Volunteer Programs

Again, this is something that is a matter of opinion and should be taken as a general rule of thumb rather than something that's true for all programs. When I first started thinking about traveling the world, I considered a volunteer program - a for-profit program. There are many programs that place 'volunteers' around the world to spend their time serving homeless populations, teaching English to kids, working in clinics in Africa and other altruistic endeavours. But, they ask for payment, usually upwards of a thousand dollars per week which, of course, does not include airfare and may even require you to pay for your own meals. The reasoning behind it is that the money is then used towards the host family (which is reasonable) and towards program expenses and insurance. But how many expenses can an organization or a family have in a third world country where the cost of living is incredibly cheap? The costs are steep and it begs the question: how much is being used to actually serve the people and used on volunteers, rather than fattening the paychecks of those involved in the for-profit volunteer business?

It's important to do your research should you decide to pursue this endeavour, but I would recommend going the independent route. Look up clinics online in places and towns you'd like to travel. Don't rely on an organization that profits off your generosity. Instead, use Helpx.net (which, yes, does require an initial but small membership fee) to find a volunteer position that is free. Search online and avoid scams that ask for money. Ultimately, your relentless labor should be enough to cover any living expenses. If you're volunteering 40 hours per week, you are paying with your invaluable time and shouldn't have to pay thousands of dollars to serve. There are several organizations that exist, primarily in the medical field and English teaching industry, that would be happy to work with you. Many of the legitimate nonprofits and NGOs around the world would likely help work something out with you in the way of accommodation arrangements.

Stay Clear of Costly Volunteer Programs and Religious Trips

Ultimately, you should be in control of your experience and shouldn't be pressured by religious groups on what you can and can't do. If you want to partake in a Buddhist meditation ceremony or travel to Mecca, that's totally fine, no matter what religion you subscribe to. Also, travel should never drain you financially - especially when you are volunteering your time and energy into creating strong, healthy communities abroad. If you really want to help others abroad, be sure to research local clinics, orphanages, animal shelters on HelpX or Workaway.info and see if they take international volunteers. Find out if they have any free housing programs in exchange for your labor. While volunteering and mission trips can be amazing experiences, you want to travel as much as deeply as possible; that's not going to happen on these restrictive types of trips. And if you raise several thousands of dollars, you want to ensure it's allocated correctly. Your best bet is to travel for free in exchange for your help via HelpX or Workaway, or even the Peace Corps!

The Time to Shine Your Light in the World Is Now

Now that we have explored the many ways you can pair your passion to help better the world with free travel, you should start looking further into these programs now. Don't hold back and don't put it off any longer; you could be the type of person who's needed halfway around the world! Since these programs are almost entirely free, you should have no fears of making the leap. With these methods, you won't be living a lavish life whatsoever (if you're looking for ways to make money as you travel, download my other book "Laptop Entrepreneur: Realistic Ways You Can Live the Dream Abroad as a Digital Nomad and Make Money Online") but these opportunities will earn you the opportunity of seeing the world for free while helping people in completely different corners of the world. There's a program for everyone - whether you're interested in working with wildlife or teaching English to kids, you'll find your place in one of the programs I mentioned.

There are even options within the USA that you may not have considered, like joining the AmeriCorps program in order to serve the American population domestically. Who says travel has to be leaving the country? Why not trade the East Coast for the West, or vice-versa, or head down south if you're in the north or even head to the rural suburbs if you're in the city with these programs? No matter where you end up along your journey, I hope you choose to put your passions first and surrender to your wanderlust.

Just Go!

I was 18 years old when I hopped on a plane by myself from Hawaii to Tokyo. I was the only non-Japanese person on the plane, I don't speak Japanese, I was a little jaded and was already slightly shocked and mesmerized as a foreign tongue and people surrounded me. That's when I started to think to myself "What did I get myself into? Am I really doing this?" I started having regrets and fears. But, here I am. I survived and I can tell you now that I don't regret that decision at all. In fact, that moment I pushed myself out of the nest was one of the best moments in my life. I decided to soar rather than cave in to doubts and worries. It made me more confident and aware of myself and the world, and I want this for you too. The first step is always the hardest. You may be scared, overwhelmed, and filled with doubts and emotions about giving up everything and packing your bags once you've found the perfect volunteer opportunities. But trust me, you just need to go. Trust in yourself, trust the process and trust the hundreds of thousands of travellers all around the world who have decided to volunteer abroad - you can be one of them, too! The point is you need to act now an tak proactive steps. Instead of letting these words go in one year and out the other, visit the websites I mentioned. Highlight your favorite opportunities. Create a deadline and apply to some programs by then. Share your goals (and this book!) with your friends - then, make them happen!

Traveling is like going down those steep black water slides at the waterpark (you know the one I'm talking about!) If you're scared of heights like me, you probably shake at the thought of reaching the top of the stairs. But when you take that 'step' and decide to just go for it with an ounce of courage, you'll start to feel overwhelmed with euphoria as you slide down that slide, experiencing a sensation you've never felt before in your life. Exhilaration, high, fear. All at once. That's what travel is like. Travel is all about reaching new boundaries within as you explore the world that surrounds you.

It may sound crazy - but just go! That's my best advice. Like a mother bird pushing her young out of a nest, you need to take a leap of faith and trust that everything will be OK. It may seem scary - what if you fail? - but, with the right planning and acceptance into some of the aforementioned programs or participation in a volunteer program, you'll be able to travel the world for virtually zero dollars and live a passion-focused life rather than a mundane one. If travel has been on your heart and mind for a while, it's time to take the idea of traveling the world from the backburner of your mind and shift it to the forefront. You have the power to make real change around you - both in your local community and wherever your travels take you. If you can't shake your wanderlust and would like to pair travel with volunteering, I encourage you to act now and be the change you wish to see in the world.

Discover More

Thank you so much for buying this book. Since I'm a self-publisher, I'd greatly appreciate it if you could spread the word - if you enjoyed this book, leave me a quick review on Amazon and share this book with friends or on social media. I've also written the following books to help others travel and become Digital Nomads:

- **Journey On:** How To Travel The World — Even If You're Young And Broke
- **Laptop Entrepreneur:** Realistic Ways You Can Live the Dream Abroad as a Digital Nomad and Make Money Online

If you'd like to reach out to me or hire me for any copywriting, digital marketing, eCommerce, or search engine optimization (SEO) projects, visit www.ryanscottseo.com.

Works Cited

"ABOUT WWOOF." *WWOOF*, wwoof.net/.

"AmeriCorps." *Corporation for National and Community Service*, www.nationalservice.gov/programs/americorps.

Bloom, Laura Begley. "23 Companies That Help You Travel The World For Free (And Might Pay You, Too)." *Forbes*, Forbes Magazine, 30 Sept. 2019, www.forbes.com/sites/laurabegleybloom/2016/07/27/23-companies-that-will-help-you-travel-the-world-for-free-and-maybe-even-pay-you-to-do-it/.

"Latest Videos." *Help Exchange: Free Volunteer Work Exchange Abroad Australia New Zealand Canada Europe*, www.helpx.net/.

"NCCC Benefits." *Corporation for National and Community Service*, www.nationalservice.gov/programs/americorps/americorps-programs/americorps-nccc/nccc-benefits.

Scott, Matt. "10 Volunteer Opportunities for Free Travel." *Matador Network*, 19 Aug. 2013, matadornetwork.com/change/10-volunteer-opportunities-for-free-travel/.

"Workaway in over 180 Countries - Give Meaning to Your Travels." *Workaway.info the Site for Cultural Exchange. Gap Year Volunteer for Food and Accommodation Whilst Travelling Abroad.*, www.workaway.info/.

Made in the USA
Las Vegas, NV
07 November 2021

33921462R00067